Deepfakes

DEEPFAKES

Graham Meikle

polity

First published in 2023 by Polity Press

Polity Press
65 Bridge Street
Cambridge CB2 1UR, UK

Polity Press
111 River Street
Hoboken, NJ 07030, USA

ISBN-13: 978-1-5095-4820-0
ISBN-13: 978-1-5095-4821-7 (pb)

A catalogue record for this book is available from the British Library.

Library of Congress Control Number: 2022934669

Typeset in 11 on 13 pt Sabon
by Fakenham Prepress Solutions, Fakenham, Norfolk NR21 8NL
Printed and bound in Great Britain by TJ Books Ltd, Padstow, Cornwall

The publisher has used its best endeavours to ensure that the URLs for external websites referred to in this book are correct and active at the time of going to press. However, the publisher has no responsibility for the websites and can make no guarantee that a site will remain live or that the content is or will remain appropriate.

Every effort has been made to trace all copyright holders, but if any have been overlooked the publisher will be pleased to include any necessary credits in any subsequent reprint or edition.

For further information on Polity, visit our website:
politybooks.com

Contents

Acknowledgements

Thanks for all kinds of things to Chris Atton, Eddy Borges-Rey, Mercedes Bunz, Steve Collins, Mary Kay Culpepper & Cullen Clark, Jennifer Fraser, Athina Karatzogianni, Tama Leaver, Louise Murray, Eduardo Navas, Michaela O'Brien, Didem Özkul, Michael Scott & Jorge Chamizo, Phaedra Shanbaum, Pieter Verdegem, Sherman Young, and the lockdown Fridays groupchat crew.

Thanks to Mary Savigar, Stephanie Homer, Justin Dyer, and everyone at Polity for their enthusiasm, patience, and professionalism.

Special thanks to Fin, Rosie, and Lola for being real.

Introduction

Did you see that video of Kim Kardashian? The one where she says, 'I genuinely love the process of manipulating people online for money'? How about the clips of Facebook's Mark Zuckerberg where he says that he has 'total control of billions of people's stolen data', and that 'the more you express yourself, the more we own you'? Or did you see the video of Donald Trump reading kids a Christmas story about a heroic reindeer that gets cheated out of winning an election? Maybe you saw the one of Vladimir Putin dismissing claims he was interfering in US democracy by saying, 'I don't have to – you are doing it to yourselves.' Then again, he was also in that video with all the world leaders singing John Lennon's 'Imagine' together. That one was nice. Perhaps you saw that clip of artist Marcel Duchamp already talking about Big Data way back in the 1950s. That was quite a find. Or that video of David Beckham appealing for support in nine different languages in the campaign to eradicate malaria? If you watch his lips, it looks like he can really speak them all. Or maybe you've heard whispers that there's a website with hundreds of porn videos starring all the

big thing about deepfakes

1

actors from the Marvel films. Those can't be real. Can they?

Those are all examples of *deepfakes*: videos created or manipulated using artificial intelligence (AI) techniques. Show the software enough photos of Scarlett Johansson, Donald Trump, or yourself and it can generate entirely new video images of those people in simulated situations. Any individual can be shown saying things they have never said and doing things they have never done. Deepfakes are an unprecedented convergence of AI, social media, political communication, pornography, media manipulation, and remix aesthetics. The uses of deepfakes offer enormous creative potential but also threaten many different kinds of harm. Deepfakes can circulate through social media, so we may never be certain of a clip's original source or of why it is in our feed. They can be harmful to all of us as individual viewers or audiences when they are created to be manipulative and deceptive. They may seek to confuse, exploit, and distort our attitudes and perceptions. Deepfakes are also often harmful to their targets: those whose faces are manipulated into new contexts, particularly pornographic ones, can experience irreparable damage to their reputations and personal lives. Deepfakes, moreover, may be harmful to society as a whole, further weakening trust in public communication and institutions, and enabling new levels of cynicism and mistrust. What happens when we can no longer trust that what we see is real?

This book explains what deepfakes are, and explores the main ways they have been used so far. Deepfakes simulate people's faces and voices in believable ways. They are examples of the larger area of *synthetic media*, those created or significantly altered by AI techniques. Synthetic media is an expanding category:

how they can effect

Introduction

There are many kinds of synthetic media, and the field is constantly expanding to include image and text generation, music composition, and voice production. Just as with legacy technologies, the use or application of synthetic media can be for the civic good or societal harm. There is increasing interest in using synthetic media for art, urban planning, environmental science, and health care. (Ajder & Glick 2021: 9)

So deepfakes should be understood first as part of this emerging field of synthetic media. They can also be understood as part of a broad spectrum of the production and manipulation of images, audio, and video (Paris & Donovan 2019). This can include sophisticated uses of AI machine-learning tools to generate or edit videos, images, or audio. But this spectrum can also include technically simple processes such as slowing down a video to make a speaker appear drunk or confused. For this reason, some commentators contrast the term *deepfakes* with other terms such as *cheap fakes* (Paris & Donovan 2019) or *shallowfakes* (Ajder et al. 2019) to emphasize the AI dimension to synthetic media. But it's more useful to line these things up together on a spectrum than it is to draw distinctions based on technical production methods. The importance of seeing deepfakes as part of a much wider continuum of synthetic, manipulated, or remixed media is that this allows for both historical perspective and cultural context. There has been image manipulation for as long as there have been images, and we can take lessons from this to help us understand contemporary deepfakes.

This is one of the first books to study synthetic media from humanities and social sciences perspectives, and synthetic media are going to be with us for a long time. Synthetic media are the first manifestations of using AI

3

to create media content. Deepfakes are the first uses of synthetic media to attract attention. This is a fast-moving area, so some of the examples explored in this book may date quickly, while others are likely to persist as landmarks in synthetic media development for a long time to come. I hope the reader can look beyond the examples and find ideas in this book that they will be able to apply to new examples that emerge as deepfakes continue to develop. Mark Weiser once wrote: 'The most profound technologies are those that disappear' (1991: 94). By *disappear,* he meant they become taken for granted: electricity, for example, which we only notice if the power goes off. Weiser observed that such technologies 'weave themselves into the fabric of everyday life until they are indistinguishable from it' (1991: 94). AI and synthetic media are not yet at this point. So this is an important moment to catch deepfakes and examine them before they begin to seem normal, and before synthetic media become taken for granted.

Synthetic media are so far mostly *used* to create non-consensual porn, and mostly *imagined* to be used in politics and news. The very word *deepfake* works well to capture these aspects of the pornographic and the propagandistic. But synthetic media are not in themselves exclusively technologies of disinformation or sexual abuse. Synthetic media are not yet bound to a particular media form. They are not yet understood as fully a part of cinema, or of political communication, or of contemporary art, or of advertising. Porn is so far the dominant media form for deepfake applications, but this is contingent: there is no reason to think it will always be that way. In this, synthetic media should be seen in a longer-term perspective of digital media. Computer-generated imagery has never completely belonged to a particular media form, reaching various kinds of peak over several decades in music video, in Hollywood spectacle, and in videogames. In a similar way, the uses of synthetic media are still emerging and still up for grabs.

So some deepfakes act as showreels for their developers, others as warnings of the risks to democracy posed by synthetic videos of leaders with deceptive content. Some deepfakes are promotional content, whether for multi-lingual corporate presentations delivered by a single speaker, or for music videos for acts including Charli XCX, Paul McCartney, and Kendrick Lamar, or for celebrities such as Bruce Willis to license advertisers to use his face without him having to show up to be filmed. Some are made as *what-if* entertainment, recasting Tom Cruise in *American Psycho*, Brad Pitt as Luke Skywalker, or swapping Heath Ledger's Joker with Joaquin Phoenix's. Some deepfakes are made as contemporary art, sponsored and exhibited by museums and festivals. Such processes are rapidly being domesticated and are by no means confined to high-end art museums. Powerful open-source software such as DeepFaceLab is freely available through developers' portal Github, although this requires some skill to use in a convincing way. And at the cruder end of the spectrum are smartphone face-swap apps, such as FaceApp or Zao, that allow users to remix faces or edit themselves into movie scenes, or novelty filters on everyday apps such as Snapchat.

In this book, I argue that deepfake videos are not just significant in their own right, they also offer important insights into the wider digital media environment of the 2020s. Deepfakes did not just happen to emerge in the time of social media, but are a product of those media. The limitless datasets of images, video, text, and audio

5

that we have created through two decades of sharing on social media platforms have become raw material that enable machine-learning researchers to train AI systems to recognize, classify, and recreate images. With enough training, such systems can generate entirely new images: copies that have no original. Deepfakes expand the social media environment in which the public and the personal converge. They are a logical extension of those social media business models in which all human experience becomes content to be shared, data to be exploited. Thinking about deepfakes allows for a new perspective on the taken-for-granted nature of contemporary digital media in which our capacity to create and share increasingly conflicts with our capacity to *trust*.

Trust is central to ideas of communication and community. Trust is fundamental to developing and maintaining a sense of community through time and across space. Trust connects with ideas of truth, belief, faith. Both news and political communication are built through mechanisms for the manufacture and maintenance of trust. Meanings are not just sent, they are created together with others. Trust is a central element in this creation of meaning: belief in the reliability of a message; confidence in its truth; recourse perhaps to faith. Without trust, communication breaks down. In the networked digital environment of the 2020s, our ability to trust is confronted by the near-ubiquitous capacity to remix and share media material. Deepfakes are a significant development in the wider erosion of trust which is affecting experiences of political communication, news, and social media. A key problem for trust in the contemporary media environment is the ways in which *consent* is being withdrawn or becoming meaningless. Everyone's face, everyone's image, indeed all human experience, is now reusable as media content.

how they do it

Introduction

This is an extension and expansion of the social media business model that was established in the first two decades of the twenty-first century. As it has developed, ever more aspects of private daily life have been appropriated as public data.

In an earlier book (Meikle 2016), I described social media as the sharing industry, noting how the continual emphasis on pushing users to share more photos, more friendships, more opinions, more emotions, and on further pushing users to recirculate those things as they were posted by their friends, had become a central business model of networked digital media. The sharing industry is typified by Meta/Facebook and Alphabet/Google, and by the subsidiary elements of their digital empires, Instagram and YouTube. The same remorseless logics of data creation, capture, and circulation are also engines of the other digital behemoths – Apple and Amazon and Microsoft, Tencent and Alibaba and Baidu – and of other leading players from Twitter to Spotify, Netflix to TikTok.

In a subsequent book about the internet of things, co-written with digital theorist Mercedes Bunz (Bunz & Meikle 2018), we traced how this business model was being expanded into ever more intimate parts of everyday experience: how we were no longer pushed to share just our photos and address books, but also our shopping lists, our daily step-counts, our sleeping patterns, our calorie and alcohol intakes, our hormone cycles and heart-rates. The point was that none of this had ever been mediated before, and that this was exactly why it was of interest and value to the sharing industry.

As this invasive practice of everyday life has become more familiar and more taken for granted, so the cultural lines for its acceptance have shifted. It has become normal, if not yet natural, to yield up ever more

7

access to ever more aspects of our lives. The kind of consent that we give in clicking through screens is not meaningful, but once given it means that we did not say no. Surveillance is no longer just the domain of the state, but instead we are developing what David Lyon (2018) describes as a *culture* of surveillance. This share-and-share-alike environment of behavioural profiling and commercial targeting creates the conditions for deepfakes: anyone's face is now just more zeros and ones; any new context in which that face can be put is just more content; anything at all is just there to be taken, to be used.

So deepfakes reveal something much more general about our contemporary digital condition. It is not just superstar actors who are being objectified and manipulated, but all of us. It is not just that we are reduced to our data, but worse than that: we are reduced to other people's data. Deepfakes show us the contours of the environment in which we all now live. It is an environment in which resistance and consent to digital exploitation are both being made meaningless. An environment in which all human experience is just content and data to be manipulated and remixed.

Approaches

Deepfakes are about creating something new from existing material: about editing, manipulating, juxta-posing, connecting, counterpointing, or subverting images, audio and video. So when I began researching deepfakes, I first thought of this book as one about remix. I've always been fascinated by the kinds of creativity that are made possible by putting together things that already exist, particularly when this is done

how it use personal data

for satirical or subversive reasons (Meikle 2002, 2007), and I first wrote about remix in 2008 (Meikle 2008). One way of approaching deepfakes is to connect them with wider currents of remix creativity, and how this is now a central part of everyday digital life. Think of the ways that daily use of social media involves making new meanings by reworking found material, whether running pictures through filters or setting links in new contexts. Thinking of deepfakes as remixes connects them with prehistories of pranks and parodies, of hoaxes and satires, that go back decades. It also opens up darker prehistories of image manipulation, propaganda, and disinformation.

In this book, I use the terms *remix* and *manipulate* to describe the same processes of deepfake media. Both words describe ways of creating with found material, but I distinguish between them to discuss different topics in the following chapters. I write about *remix* when the focus is on art, creativity, education, satire, or entertainment. I write about *manipulation* when the focus is on disinformation or non-consensual porn. This distinction between *remixed* and *manipulated* media is to avoid ambiguity in the discussions of topics that might seem to have creative potential (remix) or potential for harm (manipulation).

Questions of remix became central to digital media and web cultures early in the twenty-first century. Ideas about remix cultures drew upon collage aesthetics and theories from throughout the arts and literature of the twentieth century: concepts of appropriation, of subversive juxtaposition, and of creative combination, from cinema editing, from visual arts, from modernist literature, and from improvisational music from jazz to DJ cultures. All of these cultural currents converged with digital technologies as the millennium turned, and the consolidation of the web and other digital media found expression in DIY cultures, tactical media, culture jamming, Web 2.0, and user-generated content, along with attempts to imagine new approaches to intellectual property that could accommodate these, such as Creative Commons (Navas, Gallagher & burrough 2015a: 1).

Theorists such as Lev Manovich (2001, 2006, 2007), Paul D. Miller (DJ Spooky) (2004), and Lawrence Lessig (2004, 2008) started to develop new approaches to cultural production, distribution, and reception that addressed questions of remix. Lessig built a series of influential arguments around grassroots creativity, digital technologies, and intellectual property. Riffing on the computing term 'read-only', he argued that the mass media environment of the twentieth century had been a read-only culture in which most media involved a small number of people talking to much larger audiences, and that the new century could instead be 'both read and write' (2004: 37). Like Lessig, Miller approached remix as creativity. Both considered the ethical dimensions of remix, sampling, or appropriation. In Lessig's analysis, this was about intellectual property and the need to reform stifling copyright regimes in order to foster grassroots creativity (2008). In Miller's, it was about cultural recognition: he called sampling 'ancestor worship' (2004: 65) and asked, 'Who speaks through you?' (2004: 37).

As early as 2006, Manovich could already observe that: 'It has become a cliché to announce that "we live in remix culture"' (2006: 209). The way beyond that cliché was to theorize remix more precisely, and a new area of remix *studies* began to coalesce around this project as a loose academic discourse orbiting concepts of creativity, cultural (re)production, ethics,

10

activism, and copyright (Sinnreich 2010; Navas 2012; Ferguson 2015; Gunkel 2016). Much of the literature on remix is normative and celebratory, often crossing into advocacy (see, for example, many of the essays collected in Navas, Gallagher & burrough 2015 and 2018b). Lots of the remix studies literature is rooted in fan cultures; in defending practices of pastiche and *détournement* as both artistically and ethically valid; in arguing for the rights of the fan or grassroots creator over the corporation; in defending remixes against intellectual property laws or other conceptions of authorial creativity. 'Appropriation is activism', as one remix scholar puts it (Russell 2015: 217). But deepfakes push the limits of this discourse. A non-consensual deepfake porn video of an actor from a Marvel movie is recognizably within the video remix currents of the last twenty years, but can't be defended with the same arguments about creativity, ethics, or intellectual property. So how can ideas of remix help us understand deepfakes? Think of it this way: to remix is to create with found material, and with deepfakes the found material is *us*.

To explain how deepfakes can be understood as remixes, and why this matters, I want to compare two important remix art projects, one from the emergent phase of remix cultures at the start of the twenty-first century – *Rebirth of a Nation* by Paul D. Miller – the other from the emergent phase of deepfakes at the start of the 2020s – *Warriors* by artist James Coupe. *Rebirth of a Nation* is a multimedia remix first performed in 2004 (http://djspooky.com/rebirth-of-a-nation). It's a transformative edited version of D.W. Griffith's 1915 feature film *The Birth of a Nation*, which was itself celebrated for its influential editing, its use of parallel narratives, and its array of novel cinematic transitions and shot techniques. Griffith's multiple storylines trace the introduction of slavery to America, the US Civil War, the assassination of President Lincoln, and the rise of the Ku Klux Klan in the post-war Reconstruction period. A huge success in its day, Griffith's film is largely unwatchable for many twenty-first-century viewers for its overt racism, its casting of white actors in blackface, and its depiction of the Ku Klux Klan as heroic. These have been controversial throughout the film's history: in 1956, Situationists Guy Debord and Gil Wolman used *The Birth of a Nation* as an example to introduce their concept of *détournement*. They proposed that Griffith's film should be subverted by 'adding a soundtrack that made a powerful denunciation of the horrors of imperialist war and of the activities of the Ku Klux Klan, which are continuing in the United States even now' (Debord & Wolman 2009 [1956]: 37). DJ Spooky's remix project does exactly that.

Rebirth of a Nation presents a highly abridged version of Griffith's three-hour film, edited to emphasize its most racist elements, bringing into focus the blackface performances and the depiction of the Klan. Animated overlays and on-screen diagrams highlight specific characters or impose new perspectives on scenes. The many intertitles through which Griffith delivers much narrative exposition are remixed to credit the film to Paul D. Miller with a PDM logo. There is a film version available as a DVD, but each live performance is also a remix of this version itself, and of its accompanying score, composed by DJ Spooky and recorded by the Kronos Quartet, which he remixes in real time onstage to draw on the moment and the space of the performance. Miller described his project to one film scholar as a 'digital exorcism' intended to drain Griffith's images of their power by making them 'absurd' (McEwan

2015: 89). In its complexity and ambition, *Rebirth* is a powerful example of twenty-first-century remix cultures, bringing digital techniques and sensibilities to bear on a landmark text of early cinema. It is creativity that very explicitly works with found material: Griffith's film. To see how deepfakes can also be understood as remix texts, but with a crucial twist, let's compare this example with a more recent one.

Warriors is a deepfake art installation by James Coupe, exhibited at New York's International Center of Photography in 2020 (http://jamescoupe.com/?p=2658). The project draws upon Walter Hill's 1979 feature film *The Warriors* by remixing the faces of visitors to the exhibit into scenes from Hill's movie. The original film tells the story of the eponymous street gang, who have to fight their way from one end of New York to the other after being falsely accused of murdering another gang leader, Cyrus. Incensed by Cyrus's death, every street gang in the city is out for revenge on the Warriors, and much of the film is set-piece encounters with other gangs, many based around particular demographic characteristics, such as the all-Black Riffs or the all-female Lizzies. Visitors to Coupe's installation are invited to use one of a set of iPads around the room to take photos of their own face, which are analysed and mapped by deep learning software. The visitors' faces are then assigned to individual characters from different gangs in Hill's movie, and appear remixed into scenes from the film on screens throughout the exhibition space.

Coupe's project uses deepfake technology to explore questions of identity, visibility, profiling, and algorithmic bias. The artwork profiles each individual participant and reduces them to certain demographic characteristics. But the visitor has no way of knowing what criteria the system uses in assigning them to a particular group of characters from the movie. In a filmed interview, Coupe explains how his system uses the ImageNet dataset to categorize faces:

> ImageNet is one of the most prominent image classifiers used by AI systems. It's a dataset of over 14 million images that have been manually annotated by crowd workers. And when an AI model gets trained on ImageNet, it can look at a photo of a person and decide how to label them. It might see them as a cheerleader or a protester or a senator, based upon the photo's similarity to the images in the categories defined by ImageNet. So, in other words, these systems reproduce historical bias at a mass scale. (WITNESS 2020a)

I contrast *Warriors* and *Rebirth of a Nation* as representing two distinct historical moments of remix. The distance between these moments is fundamental to deepfakes. DJ Spooky's artwork remixes existing media content with his own musical counterpoint, and recuts Griffith's film to find and suggest new meanings. It's an example of remix as creating-with-found-material, in which that found material is other media texts. James Coupe's *Warriors* project also does this, remixing Walter Hill's 1979 movie. But *Warriors* has a very important difference that is central to the digital media environment of the 2020s. Coupe is not just remixing a text, but is also remixing its audience. The viewer's own face becomes the remixed text. The found material that is remixed and reused here is *us*.

Deepfake videos reveal how today's networked digital media systems take each of us as individuals and process us into data. We are analysed, classified, and profiled with every daily interaction, and the systems that do

14

this run on algorithmic processes that are not open or transparent. Such processes can reinforce and amplify existing social biases and inequalities (Noble 2018; Crawford 2021). What happens to the gallery visitor's face in Coupe's *Warriors* parallels the broader social uses of datasets of images in facial recognition systems. These systems encode existing social inequalities of gender, ethnicity, or class into technologies of visibility. In doing this, these processes remix us: they take our lives and identities as raw material and create us anew as profiled data subjects. What gets remixed now is not just old movies, but you and me.

Synthetic media involve sophisticated uses of AI and machine-learning technologies to create entirely new material or to rework existing material in ways that are not possible otherwise. Manipulated media are texts or images that have been edited, remixed, recontextualized. This may be for commercial reasons or for political ones, or both. There are long prehistories here, of propaganda and subversion, of collage and cut-and-paste cultures. Manipulated media need not involve sophisticated machine-learning systems or neural networks – a pair of scissors will do. I approach both synthetic and manipulated media in this book as practices of remix, of creating with found material.

In one of the first important research reports on deepfakes, Britt Paris and Joan Donovan (2019) map out a spectrum of technical sophistication that they describe as 'The Deepfakes/Cheap Fakes Spectrum'. The more technical expertise and computing resources are required, the further an audio-visual example moves towards the *deepfake* end of the spectrum; the more technically simple and accessible, the more it moves towards the *cheap fakes* end. In this analysis, the deepfakes end of the spectrum includes:

15

- virtual performances, such as those used in major Hollywood productions to reanimate dead actors;
- face-swapping, such as the celebrity pornography that first produced the word *deepfake*;
- voice synthesis, such as that used to resurrect US President Richard Nixon to deliver a speech about the Apollo 11 space mission that was never recorded in his lifetime; or
- lip-synching, such as the video produced for BuzzFeed using the voice talents of actor Jordan Peele to simulate Barack Obama describing Donald Trump as a 'total and complete dipshit'.

It is this more technically sophisticated and adept end of the spectrum that I describe in this book as *synthetic media*.

The *cheap fakes* end of Paris and Donovan's spectrum features what I describe in this book as *manipulated* media and it includes:

- changing the context of an image or video;
- cutting-and-pasting elements of an image or video;
- speeding up or slowing down video, using basic consumer software;
- using consumer software tools or social media platforms to edit or augment an image, as in Instagram or Snapchat filters.

The categories here are not absolute. The middle of the spectrum, in particular, is blurry, as some effects at the higher end can be achieved with consumer-level software such as Adobe After Effects. But the crucial point is to set high-level technical accomplishments in synthetic media production within a cultural context that makes them intelligible.

the cutaway's

Introduction

Overview

I'm a professor of communication and digital media, subjects that are part of both the humanities and the social sciences, and so those are the perspectives from which I come to the topic of deepfakes. This is not a book of computer science. So in Chapter 1, 'What Are Deepfakes?', I set out how I use certain key words in this book, and how these are essential to an understanding of deepfake video as media. First, I outline how some everyday words such as *communication, media*, and *digital* are used in the following chapters, and how they are necessary to an understanding of deepfakes. We can best understand deepfakes if we set them in a broader context of currents and prehistories of manipulated and remixed media, not all of which need leading-edge AI technology. And second, I explain the uses of some essential terms for deepfakes that are so far less familiar when we talk about our daily lived experiences of media and communication, such as *neural network* and *machine learning*. Chapter 1 is essential to understanding what deepfakes are and sets up the detailed discussions of concrete examples that follow in the rest of the book. The reader who is curious to get to those discussions and to read about case studies of deepfake communities, creators, and videos may want to start by reading ahead to Chapter 2 or 3 before returning to Chapter 1 for more detail on how those videos have been made. (Books are still linear even in the digital age, but that doesn't mean we have to read them that way.)

Chapter 2, 'Synthetic Porn', explores what is by far the largest use of deepfakes to date. Large online communities are sharing and collaborating on the creation of synthetic videos of female celebrities, in which the face of a singer or actor is digitally manipulated onto the body of a performer in an actual porn video. This chapter focuses on a case study of one specific website dedicated not only to posting celebrity deepfake porn, but also to sharing training resources for those who want to learn how to make their own. Celebrities were the first victims of this kind of abuse, but it has already spread to affect ordinary individuals as the technology becomes domesticated and easier to use. So Chapter 2 also discusses some developments, apps, and websites that take the risks and harms of synthetic porn into everyday life. Synthetic porn videos reduce the individual victim to their digital data in a way that shows just how much contemporary digital media also enable parallel processes in everyday life. Non-consensual deepfake porn follows logically from social media business models where all human experience is nothing but data to be pillaged and exploited in the pursuit of advertising revenue.

In Chapter 3, 'Remix Aesthetics and Synthetic Media', I examine some important examples of synthetic media art and entertainment. When we start to explore different uses of these technologies, we discover that synthetic media are not necessarily *fake*, in the sense of exploitative or malicious. Journalist Nina Schick, author of one of the first books about deepfakes, suggests that 'When used maliciously as disinformation, or when used as misinformation, a piece of synthetic media is called a "deepfake"' (2020: 9). But many synthetic videos are produced for legitimate and pro-social reasons, including education, media literacy, and art. And in many cases, those creators choose to use the term *deepfake* to describe their work. Chapter 3 discusses work by leading synthetic media artists Bill Posters and Daniel Howe, *South Park* creators Trey

[margin note: what each chapter is]

Parker and Matt Stone, and documentary filmmaker David France, whose *Welcome to Chechnya* is an extraordinary example of the uses of deepfake technologies for progressive political ends. Chapter 3 also explores the synthetic media afterlife of Salvador Dalí. With the exception of David France, who offers the term *deeptruth*, all of these projects are described as deepfakes by their creators (and the same is true of other progressive projects discussed below in Chapter 4).

Chapter 3 also traces connections between contemporary uses of synthetic media for parody and satire and twentieth-century art movements, particularly Dada. It explores parallels between their different uses of found material for creative expression. This chapter also discusses the self-reflexive nature of much synthetic media content: deepfake videos that are created to draw attention to the possibilities of deepfake videos. I also expand in this chapter on the overall argument that deepfakes are a logical extension of contemporary digital media business models and cultural practices rather than some aberrant side-effect. We need to understand deepfakes not as niche or esoteric experimental AI, but as part of central currents of daily digital life.

The theme of Chapter 4 is 'Manipulating Trust'. For Christmas 2020, UK broadcaster Channel 4 created a deepfake alternative message to the nation from the Queen, who spoke about her family and showed off the dance moves from her latest TikTok video. This was deepfake-as-novelty, but the script did return more than once to the significant theme of trust: 'If there is a theme to my message today, it is trust. Trust in what is genuine – and what is not' and 'So much of our world today comes to us through these screens, which brings me back to that question of trust, of whether what we see and hear is always as it seems.' Chapter 4 explores this theme of trust. Deepfakes have created some anxiety and considerable hype around their potential to destabilize political communication. They are seen as contributing to the erosion of trust that already affects some countries' political and media systems.

The standard fear raised is that a deepfake of a political leader could precipitate an actual crisis, if believed to be real by enough people in a dangerous enough context and moment. But the more visible trend is in fact towards using political deepfakes to promote media literacy: synthetic videos of Vladimir Putin, Boris Johnson, Barack Obama, Kim Jong-un, and other leaders have been produced as initiatives in trying to make publics aware of the risks of deepfakes. Such media literacy, though, also increases scepticism of media content, and risks deepening cynicism and undermining public trust in political communication. Legal scholars Bobby Chesney and Danielle Citron (2019) identified the problem they call the Liar's Dividend, through which public awareness of the possibility of deepfakes makes it easy for real content to be falsely dismissed as fake. Chapter 4 traces the roles of digital and social media in deepening this erosion of public trust, and it explores a number of case studies and projects in order to establish how synthetic media are being used to both corrode and encourage trust in public communication. These include 'Deep Reckonings', a conceptual project by Stephanie Lepp that uses deepfakes to simulate moments of contrition from controversial public figures, and 'In Event of Moon Disaster', a landmark deepfake that won an Emmy for its reimagining of the 1969 Apollo 11 moon landing.

Finally, the concluding chapter canvasses some solutions to the problems caused by some forms of deepfakes, while emphasizing that not all synthetic media are problems. This conclusion explores whether pornographic or deceptive political deepfakes could and should be regulated. For this, I draw on Lawrence Lessig's (1999) framework of regulatory mechanisms, which includes laws, technological interventions, market approaches, and shifting social norms and public understanding.

1

What Are Deepfakes?

When Apple launched its first iPhone to use facial recognition, the company's usual theatrical event made much of the device's sophisticated array of AI applications. Apple's Tim Cook and Phil Schiller explained how its Face ID system offered facial recognition technology for unlocking the device. Their presentation showed off the phone's sophisticated TrueDepth camera system, and its use of digital imaging sensors, ambient light detection, and infrared dot-projection technology to achieve facial recognition. They also boasted of the new iPhone's use of neural networks, and demonstrated Augmented Reality applications of its facial recognition technology.

In contrast, neither man said anything about making phone calls. Indeed, it would have been surprising if phone calls had been a focus of the launch presentation, despite the word *phone* being the heart of the product's name. Contemporary smartphones are not best understood as being phones at all, and so the emphasis instead was on technological developments that might seem esoteric to many users (*neural networks?*). Smartphones recall Arthur C. Clarke's indelible observation that 'Any sufficiently advanced technology is indistinguishable from magic' (1999: 2). But what this iPhone example shows is how such sophisticated AI systems are now also very much a taken-for-granted part of everyday life and daily communication. Powerful neural networks drive the facial recognition devices that we carry around in our hands, and enable the conversational technologies that are Siri and Alexa (Bunz & Meikle 2018). AI applications such as natural language processing, speech recognition, and computer vision are now intimately bound up with our daily experiences of work, travel, shopping, entertainment, and communication (Elliott 2019, 2022).

Communication is the making of meanings. It's something everyone can do but it's also harder than it looks. We might try to nurture a particular meaning in a particular person or to blast it at a whole population. But the outcome is never certain. Meanings have to be made, in part by the creator of a message and in part by those receiving and interpreting that message. Of course, often we accept the meaning suggested by the creator of a message, by the director of a film, or the writer of a caption explaining a photograph in a news story. But this is a messy and often contested process (Hall 2019 [1973]). The very need for that photograph's caption points to some of the complexity of this process of making meanings: a photograph may not mean much without a caption to suggest how we should read it (and indeed the photo can perform the same favour for the caption). In such processes of shaping and steering and suggesting, and in the responses and interpretations of those reading, watching, or listening, is communication, the making of meanings. We don't just take meanings, we make them. Deepfakes are first of all a communication phenomenon: they are about new ways

the meaning of deep fake

23

of making meanings, and they are also about challenges to settled understandings of how meanings get made.

All the examples in that last paragraph are of mediated communication: films, photographs, and news stories. Of course, much other communication is face-to-face, involving conversation, facial expressions, gestures, and body language. Those are all activities that work best when we are in the same space together at the same time. But all of us also spend hours every day communicating across different or distant *spaces* (a Zoom chat with a friend overseas) and different *times* (catching up with that box set everyone loved last year). For this we need *media*: systems that enable us to communicate across space or across time or both (Carey 1989; Thompson 1995; Hartley 2008; Wark 2012). Those systems have economic and technological elements: media involve industries and institutions that develop to use the possibilities offered by technological innovations. Those innovations, and those industries and institutions, shape each other, as some possibilities are pursued and others excluded. Those systems also have social and regulatory dimensions, and cultural ones: particular kinds of texts, and particular kinds of audience or user behaviour, from the shared attention of a major live TV event (Dayan & Katz 1992) to the daily Babel of a trending hashtag (Losh 2020). And of course *media* can also refer to the texts or images produced by those systems. So when we talk about *synthetic media*, we can mean the images or audio or videos that are produced by AI processes. Our experiences of media and communication are changing in profound ways as AI processes for generating and acting upon data now join the more familiar media forms that I've used for examples in this paragraph.

One example that captures all the above aspects of media is the ways that social media platforms have drawn the cultural practices of their users into their business models and the further refinement of their technological interfaces. This is crucial for the development of synthetic media too. Jean Burgess and Nancy Baym show how grassroots Twitter users developed improvements, enhancements, refinements, and add-ons that came to define many of that platform's central uses, such as the hashtag, the @-reply, and the retweet: 'Even the noun "tweet" to describe a post to the site and the verb "to tweet" to describe the act of posting such a contribution were user inventions' (2020: 33). Each of those initiatives came from cultural negotiations among Twitter users as they worked out how best to use this platform to make and share meanings with others. Burgess and Baym then show how Twitter the company absorbed these grassroots practices into its business model and into the architecture of the app: by trademarking terms, encoding user workarounds as proprietary software features, and repositioning elements of everyday Twitter culture as 'engagement metrics'. Synthetic media, similarly, are being developed through networks of interactions between different kinds of users, all trying to exploit the potential of these new technological possibilities. As we will see in this book, the uses and meanings of deepfakes are being developed in particular cultural contexts, and come to embody and express particular ideas about the world. One of these ideas is that all human experience is now media content or data that can be manipulated and remixed without meaningful consent.

Digital media express media texts and images as numbers, as zeros and ones. This makes them programmable (Manovich 2001). Once an image is expressed as numbers, then we can do maths with it. We can edit it, run it through filters, copy it, share it, perform all kinds of complex algorithmic operations on that image. This enables everyday remix creativity. Social media have made the remix impulse into an everyday practice for billions of people. Choosing a filter on Instagram is a moment of remix as we rework that existing image for its new context. Sharing a video to a WhatsApp group is also a moment of remix as we move that video from one context to another, changing the meanings that can be made from both that video and that WhatsApp chat. The entire platform of TikTok can be understood as a vast remix competition.

These senses of communication, media, and digital media, then, are all necessary to understanding how deepfakes are approached in this book. All have been shaped in the twenty-first century by the convergence of media content, telecommunications, and computing (Meikle & Young 2012). Computers have grown more powerful, and more and more devices of all kinds have been connected. Media texts and images produced, circulated, and received on ubiquitous and networked digital devices have become part of everyday life in new ways. The term *Big Data* describes the sheer volume of digital data (words, sounds, images, videos). It also captures the speed at which they are created and circulated; their granular detail and capacity to identify and connect individuals; their capacity to be combined, remixed, and scaled up to new levels; and the ever-increasing computational and telecommunications power available to process them (Lupton 2020; Kitchin 2022).

A term like *Big Data* can get a bit abstract, so let's connect it to our everyday experiences. Take a selfie. An image of a human face is as simple as mediated communication gets. It combines the personal with the public expression or performance of identity. The selfie has become the signature media gesture of the twenty-first

26

century, and the major digital platforms have driven this. Social media users provide material for facial recognition technologies and proprietary databases by contributing their own pictures. From the emergence of social media profile pictures, through the introduction of smartphones with front-facing cameras, to image hashtags such as #MeAt20 or #10YearChallenge, digital media platforms have seen us editing, refining, perfecting, curating, and circulating these images we make of ourselves. We tag them and label them and add their locations.

Without us realizing, our daily social media use has provided images used to create datasets of incredible scale, diversity, and reach. These datasets can be used to train AI to recognize faces, to identify individuals, to recreate them, and, given enough examples, to generate convincing images of people who have never existed. The things we all do on social media every day create enormous quantities and varieties of data. Our smartphones are packed with sensors that monitor and track what we do and where we go, and communicate that across digital networks. These data are being used to develop machine-learning AI technologies (Bunz & Meikle 2018: 76). This is Big Data. The individual no longer needs to take any more selfies: that can now be done for them by software. The starting point to understand how these processes enable the emergence of deepfakes, and how deepfakes connect with more everyday experiences of media and communication, is the word *algorithm*.

'Fuck the algorithm'

The Covid-19 pandemic caused chaos for school exam systems across the UK. In August 2020, with A-level exams cancelled, students in England were instead given surrogate grades for those qualifications, which are the standard route to university entrance. Those grades were moderated by an algorithm that ranked their teachers' predictions of their marks against their schools' performances in previous years. The outcomes were widely seen as unfair, with 40% of teachers' predicted marks downgraded. As a result, many thousands of prospective students, and their intended universities, found their plans for the coming academic year shredded. Crowds of young people protested in the streets, chanting 'Fuck the algorithm'. The algorithm itself took on a role as lead character in many news stories: the prime minister blamed the chaos on 'a mutant algorithm', while the BBC headlined a report on its website 'Why did the A-level algorithm say no?' (Coughlan 2020).

This was the wrong question. Such algorithms do what they're programmed to do, so the question should have been 'Why was the algorithm told to say no?' The exams fiasco was a social and political failure, not a technological one. A basic algorithm like the one used to amend those young people's qualifications is not a magic spell, but is better understood as something more like a recipe: a set of rules and instructions for the completion of a specific computing or mathematical procedure. But like all analogies, this is of course an inexact comparison. So you might improvise a little while cooking from a recipe, but a computer algorithm requires precision. A computer algorithm, explains Thomas Cormen (2013: 1), 'is a set of steps to accomplish a task that is described precisely enough that a computer can run it'.

In the networked digital media environment, algorithms are ever more central to everyday life and communication. They are used to profile individuals and to evaluate relevance, their use at the same time promising mathematical objectivity and offering a process to blame when things go wrong (Gillespie 2016: 24). Algorithmic processes select the video that YouTube auto-plays after the one you wanted, they inform Instagram's suggestions of whom you should follow, and they determine Twitter's ordering of which tweets you see (and which ones you don't). Your Spotify, Amazon, and Netflix recommendations are calculated by algorithms, and so are your Tinder dates. Algorithms are used both as a necessary means of processing unfathomable quantities of data (Google's search results), and as an invasive means of attempting to not only predict but also influence people's behaviour (Facebook's targeted ads).

As those school students protesting in the streets show, many people know or sense that algorithms are deployed to sort and rank and predict ever more aspects of their lives. Sometimes we may directly try to make use of this: for example, by choosing to use a hashtag in order to make our post more visible to more people, in a process of algorithmic sorting (Gillespie 2014: 184). At other times, we may even directly try to interfere with these processes, resisting the ceaseless requests for more data with false information, alternate profiles, or tactical use of devices and platforms (Brunton & Nissenbaum 2015). But it is rarely clear to users *how* algorithms are set up to do all of this sorting, ranking, and predicting, or what data they are using to do it. Those algorithms, and the data and choices that inform their programming, are often opaque, and so they come to stand in for the wider social processes of which they are just one technical component (Gillespie 2016; O'Neil 2016). Evidence mounts up that algorithmic systems reinforce existing social biases:

What Are Deepfakes?

> Image recognition tools miscategorize Black faces, chatbots adopt racist and misogynistic language, voice recognition software fails to recognize female-sounding voices, and social media platforms show more highly paid job advertisements to men than to women. (Crawford 2021: 128)

The very idea of algorithms simultaneously seems to connote 'advanced technology, creepy mathematical efficacy, and shadowy control' (Seaver 2019: 412–13). So like those young people chanting in the streets, we blame the algorithm itself rather than those who design, programme, and implement it.

But digital media algorithms are no longer just used to curate, rank, classify, or predict. Deepfakes are an example of new and emerging kinds of *synthetic media*: media texts and images that are *created* or *manipulated* by advanced algorithmic processes of *machine learning*. How does this work? Algorithms can look for, identify, and respond to patterns. They can then draw inferences from data, and change their own processes to accommodate these. Given enough data, such algorithms 'learn' or adapt to solve problems (Kitchin 2022: 100–12; Bucher 2018: 23–8). This is the basis of machine learning. Instead of programming rules that lead to a result, such as a cake as in the recipe analogy, new algorithmic rules are now themselves the result. As Mercedes Bunz explains, '[I]nstead of an algorithm written by a programmer, the programmer now sets up a framework that runs a data-analysis with the algorithm as an outcome' (2019: 264). So, for example, if the framework analyses enough images of human faces, it can develop rules – an algorithm – with which to generate new ones.

There are variations in machine learning to do with how much help the system is given. Machine learning can be *supervised*, which means the system is told what to look for, and is provided with lots of labelled and organized data as examples. Once the system can recognize some features of the original data, it can then recognize them when given new data. The process has created a rule or algorithm that the system can apply to new examples. Or machine learning can be *unsupervised*, when it is just given loads of unlabelled data and left to see what it comes up with. The value of this can be in what patterns the process discovers. Another variation is *reinforcement* learning, which works through trial and error, leading the system to learn the optimal choice in a given situation (Broussard 2018: 87–94; Devlin 2018: 78–86; Gunkel 2020: 86–7). This might be used in teaching a network to play chess or a robot to navigate its surroundings, for example (Kelleher 2019).

Machine learning is today the dominant paradigm in AI research and applications. Asking for a simple definition of AI is enough to start a fight in an empty room. One reason is that the term covers some very different things. It describes a branch of computer science, but also specific applications, and is often bound up as well with both sci-fi fantasy and marketing hype. Another reason is that *intelligence* itself is very hard to define (Warwick 2012): is it about the capacity to respond to the input of the senses, or about reason, or about learning, or about communication, for instance? Pieter Verdegem suggests as a basic definition of AI: 'computer programming that learns from and adapts to data' (2021: 5). This very clearly equates AI with machine learning, the conceptual approach that is fundamental to enabling deepfakes. Verdegem juxtaposes this initial definition with Anthony Elliott's slightly fuller explanation of AI as 'any computational

31

system that can sense its relevant context and react intelligently to data' (2019: 4). Elliott's use of *sense* here adds the important dimension of *sensors*, components of a system that detect and communicate changes in their environment (Bunz & Meikle 2018). Networked sensors – your phone is packed full of them – are one key way in which data are generated and circulated in order to be used in machine learning.

Some machine-learning processes, the previously mentioned *neural networks*, are organized around models inspired by how signals pass between neurons in the human brain (Warwick 2012: 88–101). A neural network is a combination of mathematical models arranged in layers, so that the output of each layer becomes the input of the next, allowing for increased complexity with every additional layer of computation (Bunz & Meikle 2018: 73–81; Gunkel 2020: 70–87). In the case of image recognition, for example, one layer might detect the presence of edges, before further layers identify patterns of edges that combine into familiar objects (LeCun, Bengio & Hinton 2015). These neural networks can be organized around many layers of processing and computation, allowing for processes known as *deep learning*. Deep learning is about building complex systems of neural networks that can make decisions based on data (Kelleher 2019: 1). We encounter such systems in everyday situations such as searching for an image on Google or using the facial recognition option to unlock our phones. The word *deepfake* is generally understood to be a portmanteau term that remixes the words *deep learning* with the word *fake*.

A key technique is the Generative Adversarial Network (GAN). GANs are one model often associated with the creation of synthetic media, although it is important

32

both to see the word *deepfake* as describing a spectrum of manipulated, remixed, and synthetic media, and not to over-identify deepfakes with a single technical process. GANs have been crucial to the emergence of synthetic media, and their principles are important for face-swapping videos, which are one of the fundamental forms of deepfake. A GAN puts two neural networks in competition against each other. One, known as the *generator*, is made to process thousands of examples of a particular class of images, such as human faces. It is trained to recognize and classify their elements – lips, noses, eyebrows – and to develop rules with which to recreate them. It can then use those rules to create new images that follow the rules but that are actually images of faces that have never existed – such images are examples of synthetic media. The second neural network, known as the *discriminator*, is trained to distinguish between the actual and the synthetic images, and to reject the synthetic ones (Gunkel 2020: 192–3). Ethem Alpaydin (2021) offers the useful analogy of the *generator* being an art forger that can create fake paintings and the *discriminator* being an art expert that can detect fake paintings. In this analogy, the GAN works to help the art forger to deceive the art expert. The goal of the process is to generate synthetic images that the discriminator is unable to detect – and that the human viewer will be unable to detect either.

Simone Natale (2021) argues that this kind of deception has always been at the heart of AI. Since the earliest days of computing, researchers and developers have drawn upon knowledge of users' expectations in order to present a meaningful illusion of intelligent machines. Starting with the Turing Test, in which a system is considered to be intelligent if it is able to fool humans, AI developers have assumed that the reaction

33

of human observers or participants is the measure of success. So AI research privileges developments that exploit the users' perceptions and expectations. As a result, Natale argues, we have 'the creation not of intelligent beings but of technologies that humans perceive as intelligent' (2021: 3). Alan Turing's 'Imitation Game' succeeds if the human user is deceived. It's not about whether machines exhibit intelligence but whether we believe they do. A good AI development, in this analysis, is one that fools us into thinking we are interacting with a technological entity exhibiting human intelligence.

To see if you could be deceived by the results of a trained GAN, try the website This Person Does Not Exist. The page shows a full-screen synthetic image of a human face. Every time the user reloads the page, a fresh synthetic image is generated. Most are very convincing. Some might not fool a careful human observer, particularly when the image has been distorted by some additional focus in the original image set that the GAN hasn't been trained to cope with, such as a hand on a shoulder or a head covering. But many look strikingly real. The creative possibilities are huge, and so are the possibilities for misuse. A synthetic image generator like this offers a limitless supply of potentially deceptive pictures for use in identity scams, catfishing, fake profiles, false ads, manipulative PR, and disinformation campaigns.

There is also This Person Exists, which shows images of real people whose faces have been used to train the NVidia StyleGan tool that powers This Person Does Not Exist. StyleGan has drawn upon images from social media platforms such as Flickr that were posted under Creative Commons licences, using those photos to train its neural networks. The synthetic images of This Person Does Not Exist are derived from the real faces of real people who will be unaware of their role in this project. It is difficult to imagine that those clicking to allow the Creative Commons option on their photo on Flickr over a decade ago could have envisaged their likeness being one day used to train AI tools in this way. It is not possible to give meaningful consent in clicking *OK* when we cannot imagine what future applications might exploit that consent.

AI researchers have drawn upon progressively larger databases throughout the social media era, with a clear trend towards abandoning questions of consent (Raji & Fried 2021). Researchers began to harvest faces from Google Images, Flickr, and Yahoo by the mid-2000s. In 2014, researchers at Facebook developed the DeepFace facial recognition model, trained on 4 million Facebook profile photos (Raji & Fried 2021: 3). (We'll return to Facebook's use of facial recognition technology in the concluding chapter.) The new commercial possibilities of deep learning on such vast image sets began to attract further researchers, who created further datasets and further models. Kate Crawford describes such harvesting of public data in this way:

> There has been a widespread pillaging of public spaces; the faces of people in the street have been captured to train facial recognition systems; social media feeds have been ingested to build predictive models of language; sites where people keep personal photos or have online debates have been scraped in order to train machine vision and natural language algorithms. This practice has become so common that few in the AI field even question it. (Crawford 2021: 220)

Clearview AI, for example, is a facial recognition company that says it has scraped 3 billion personal photos and video images from Facebook and YouTube without anyone's consent, and that licenses its face identification technology to hundreds of police forces and security agencies, including the FBI (Hill 2020). What we choose to share on social media can be seen as wide open for exploitation by others. All human experience is reduced to data, and all data can be exploited.

The source code used on This Person Does Not Exist is freely available, and works on any large set of images from the same class, not just human faces. The website links to others in the same series that present synthetic horses, artworks, chemical molecules, and, of course, cats. An inexhaustible supply of fresh cat pictures looks like a logical end-point for the web era. But cats are not the only inevitable content, and Rule 34 of the internet states that if something exists, then there is porn of it (Poole 2010). Rule 34 is both ironic and accurate (as evidence, there is erotic fan fiction about Marx and Engels, for instance, or a very large Reddit community dedicated to making and sharing Sonic the Hedgehog porn). So inevitably, inspired by This Person Does Not Exist, a project called These Nudes Do Not Exist emerged to generate a unique synthetic nude image for a fee of $1. Let's note something very important about this site, which will become more significant in Chapter 2. The site, now renamed Harem Token, can only generate images of naked women. It can't create synthetic nudes of men, because it has been trained on an image set of real photos only of women. This illustrates an important point about algorithmic biases and about the distortions that can be introduced by skewed data. All technologies can be understood as material expressions of social relations. They are designed and developed by particular groups of people and express those people's worldviews and assumptions in techno-logical form. 'Technology is society made durable', as Bruno Latour puts it (1991).

In Safiya Umoja Noble's book *Algorithms of Oppression*, she argues that algorithms are 'loaded with power' (2018: 171). Noble recounts how her own experiences of everyday algorithmic technology, such as search engines, showed her that algorithms come with inbuilt politics:

> While Googling things on the Internet that might be interesting to my stepdaughter and nieces, I was overtaken by the results. My search on the keywords 'black girls' yielded HotBlackPussy.com as the first hit. Hit indeed. (2018: 3)

Those search algorithms were of course not designed with the explicit intention of reinforcing racist ideologies or gendered prejudices. But like any other technology, they were designed with the assumptions, worldviews, and commercial imperatives of their programmers and platforms. Moreover, in the specific case of Google's search algorithms, these build upon complex histories of the previous searches of hundreds of millions of users, and upon a weighting in search results for sites to which many other sites link. So the results both legitimize and reinforce social practices, from regulation to everyday use. As Kate Crawford puts it, 'AI systems both reflect and produce social relations and understandings of the world' (2021: 8).

Distortions such as the one Noble describes can emerge at any point in a system, from the available data (previous search results), to the ways those data are selected and processed (search algorithms), to the ways those processed data arrive anew in the world (the search results that confronted Noble). No technology is neutral. But the increasing ubiquity of algorithmic systems for sorting and ranking and predicting makes possible a deeper entrenchment of existing social inequalities. 'We have more data and technology than ever in our daily lives,' writes Noble, 'and more social, political, and economic inequality and injustice to go with it' (2018: 171).

Not all synthetic media involve creating entirely new images of non-existent things. Another approach is *face-swapping* or *face replacement*, so far most often taking the image of a female celebrity and swapping it for that of a porn performer. There are also *face re-enactment* or *puppetry* videos, in which Vladimir Putin or Tom Cruise appear to say or do things they have never said or done. And there is *speech synthesis*, which can create new human voices or emulate specific ones, such as that of a politician (CDEI 2019). As with GANs, face-swapping uses the power of two neural networks, each called an *autoencoder*, and each programmed to analyse a collection of images of a particular person. Creating this collection of images is the first step, and can be automated to use software to extract still images of the source's face from a video clip. The first autoencoder is then trained on these images of, let's say, actor Nicolas Cage shrieking about bees. Through processing thousands of images of Cage, the neural network learns to *encode* Cage's face into a basic image, and then to *decode* that image by reconstructing the original: it learns to break the face down to its simplest elements and then put it back together again. The second network uses the same encoding model to do the same process with the target face: let's say, Donald Trump shrieking about people not voting for him. Once the networks can encode and decode high-quality images of both Cage and Trump, the decoder elements are swapped, so that Cage's face is encoded using the Cage model but decoded by the Trump model. After some post-production editing, the result is Cage's face digitally stitched into a video of Trump (Zucconi 2018; CDEI 2019; Mirsky & Lee 2020).

Nancy Pelosi's drinking problem

Senior US Democrat Nancy Pelosi doesn't drink alcohol, but she does have a unique drinking problem. That problem is that people persist in circulating manipulated videos in which her speech has been edited and slowed to make her appear drunk. In early August 2020, a US election year, one video clip of an interview in which the Speaker of the House of Representatives appeared to slur her words as though intoxicated was shared more than 90,000 times on Facebook, drawing more than 2 million views. But in the original unedited video, Pelosi's speech is entirely normal (the two can be compared at Denham 2020). Some platforms, including Twitter, TikTok, and YouTube, removed the manipulated video after being contacted by CNN. But Facebook did not remove the video, instead adding a warning label that its content was 'partly false' (O'Sullivan 2020). Pelosi had also been the target of very similar attacks in May 2019, which saw prominent opponents including Donald Trump, Rudy Giuliani, and Fox News share other manipulated videos that falsely showed her slurring or stammering (Harwell 2019).

The first thing to take from the Nancy Pelosi case is its technological aspect. This was not a sophisticated use of synthetic media or GANs. This was just someone slowing down a video clip. Anyone can learn to do that from a three-minute YouTube tutorial. It needs nothing more cutting-edge than the kinds of domestic lifestyle software that come pre-installed on many laptops or phones. So on the spectrum of manipulated media, this example is towards the lower end of technical difficulty to create. The very simplicity of this helps to show the nature and scale of the problems here. Manipulating digital media images and texts is really easy, and sharing these across social media is trivial to do. Disinformation like the Pelosi video can therefore easily find significant audiences.

So this is the second thing to take from the Pelosi case: the roles of social media in the circulation of deceptive synthetic or manipulated media. The best thing about networked digital media in the twenty-first century is how easy and accessible they are to use. Anyone can say anything they want to anyone else, anywhere and anytime. But this is also the worst thing about networked digital media in the twenty-first century. Social media provide platforms for anyone to say and make things, to share the things that they and others have said and made, and to make all of this saying, making, and sharing visible to others (Meikle 2016). Over the years, new features have been introduced to make these activities easier for the user, from the automated retweet button, to the embedding of the *like* option on countless other websites, to the algorithmic editing of our timelines in an attempt to supply us with more attractive posts. The business models of Instagram or YouTube or Twitter rely on keeping the user on the app as much as possible. The platforms want the user to post, to comment, to share, because every moment of interaction creates more data that they can use to refine their behavioural profile of that individual user.

What Are Deepfakes?

As these corporations have ingested our personal lives, so making a joke, sharing a picture, or messaging a friend have been redefined as engagement metrics. And it is inimical to the platforms to do anything that reduces engagement. It is not in their commercial interest to restrict or censor content. On the contrary, the more content to which a user responds, the better for that platform. This is the kind of judgement behind Facebook's refusal to remove the Nancy Pelosi video. So we have a situation in which digital media images can be manipulated and shared from one context to another, from where they may be further shared, selected, and promoted by algorithms. As a result, the user may never be certain of quite why a video or a story appears in their feed or what its original source is, while at the same time that user is nonetheless encouraged to share it still further with their own networks. These are ideal conditions for the circulation of deepfakes.

This leads to the third thing we can take from the Pelosi example: the ongoing erosion of trust in public communication, and the complex ways in which social media enable political partisanship. These connect easily to political partisanship of all stripes. Tech culture blog Boing Boing shared a slowed-down video of Donald Trump in 2016, although its title was given as 'Trump slowed 50%', which doesn't suggest deceptive intent (Beschizza 2016). The Trump White House circulated a manipulated video of CNN reporter Jim Acosta, which had been doctored to make his interaction with an intern at a media conference falsely appear aggressive (Harwell 2018a). In August 2020, the Trump White House's social media director Dan Scavino tweeted a manipulated video of Joe Biden that falsely depicted him sleeping during a TV interview; this video edited an image of Biden into a real clip of a TV journalist trying

41

to wake singer Harry Belafonte as he slept through their interview (*Washington Post* 2020). In another example, Fox News was accused of manipulating video of Biden praising a black baseball player in order to make the President's language seem inappropriate; Fox programmes then went on to stoke controversy about the 'backlash' Biden faced as a result of Fox having aired their doctored version of his remarks (Associated Press 2021).

Questions of trust have been central to the study of mediated communication for a century: debates around public opinion and propaganda, around objectivity and bias, around persuasion and agenda-setting, around promotional cultures and tabloid cultures, around professional and citizen journalism, around ownership and spin, around witnesses and influencers. The rise of social media in the first two decades of the twenty-first century has reframed each of these debates (Jack 2017; Marwick & Lewis 2017; Wardle & Derakshan 2017; McNair 2018; Zimdars & McLeod 2020). The emergence of synthetic media is doing so again.

Summary

In this chapter, I outlined how we can understand deepfakes as media and communication phenomena. Synthetic media are an emerging area of communication, and it's important to recognize from the start that they do not necessarily have to be *fake*, if fake is to mean deliberately deceptive. Deepfakes are new ways of making and sharing meanings, as well as challenges to our understandings of how meanings get made. It's important to see deepfakes as part of the everyday social media and networked digital communication environment, rather than seeing them as more or less esoteric developments in AI. For this reason, I explained how everyday concepts such as *communication*, *media*, and *digital* are essential in understanding how deepfakes have emerged. I also explained the relevance of slightly more specialized terms, including *algorithm*, *machine learning*, and *neural network*. While the vocabulary of *machine learning* or *neural network* is not yet part of most people's everyday lives, such concepts are at the heart of what we all do all day long on our phones and on digital media platforms from Amazon to Instagram to Spotify. And all of that daily activity creates immense quantities of data that can be used in developing and training the algorithmic systems that make deepfakes possible. This chapter and the book's introduction have also introduced some important distinctions that help to shape the rest of the book: in particular, the distinctions between *synthetic*, *remixed*, and *manipulated* media. Deepfakes can best be understood if set in wider contexts of remix and manipulation, not all instances of which require sophisticated AI technologies.

2

Synthetic Porn

Marvel's *Avengers* films were a big hit with porn users. Pornhub claimed that the release of *Avengers: Infinity War* led to a 356% increase in users searching for porn featuring its characters on the website. In the days before the release of its sequel, *Avengers: Endgame*, searches on Pornhub for *Avengers*-related content increased by 2,912% – an extra 2 million searches in one week. Two weeks after that film was released, *Avengers* searches on Pornhub were 5,188% up on what they had been a month earlier, with searches for individual characters, particularly Captain Marvel, also going through the roof (Pornhub Insights 2019a). Pornhub's annual 'Year in Review' media release (Pornhub Insights 2019b) would later note that *Avengers* search terms, not even counting those for individual characters such as Black Widow, had topped 13 million searches. In other superhero universes, DC Comics' Harley Quinn character had been searched for 9 million times, with Wonder Woman drawing almost 4 million searches. Pornhub's in-house relationships counsellor Dr Laurie Betito, who features prominently on the site's 'Sexual Wellness' page, was quoted as saying: 'It's always fun to see our favorite video game or movie characters portrayed in a sexual manner' (Pornhub Insights 2019b).

But the problem is that it is not just the fictional characters who are being portrayed in this way. It is the actual actors who play them on screen. What many of those millions of users will have been looking for, and will have found, was deepfake porn of actors in the Marvel and DC movie franchises (Cole 2020a). Not Captain Marvel but Brie Larson, not Black Widow but Scarlett Johansson, not Harley Quinn but Margot Robbie, not Wonder Woman but Gal Gadot. Porn is of course a word that describes a very wide range of types of media content and imagery (Attwood 2018). So we should be specific. Deepfake porn is non-consensual sexual imagery made with synthetic media techniques. (I use the terms *non-consensual* and *involuntary* in this chapter, and never use the term *revenge porn*, because it implies a justification for the perpetrator.) A deepfake porn video of Margot Robbie's face swapped onto the body of an actual porn performer is not made with the consent of either woman. So it is a form of abuse. And as we will see in this chapter, it is a form of abuse that is no longer directed only at celebrities.

Deepfake porn may seem an extreme case, but it is an outcome of the digital business models that have shaped our contemporary media environment. Deepfake porn involves appropriating the star images (Dyer 2004) and faces of actual people, editing them into scenarios for which they have not given consent, and exhibiting the results in more or less public ways. Pornographic deepfakes take the image of the individual celebrity as an object to be not only shared but also edited and manipulated. They reduce that individual person to digital content, to raw material for a bespoke text. Celebrity and sexual fantasy have always been

45

inextricably linked. An image of Jennifer Lawrence might provide raw material for a private fantasy, but to publish a video in which her face is made to appear in actual pornography is to treat her as a different kind of raw media material. It is to reduce the individual to zeros and ones in a way that offers perspective on how contemporary digital media also enable this process across a much broader spectrum of human behaviour than just the pornographic. The involuntary deepfake is a logical extension of those social media business models in which all human experience is reduced to data to be shared in the pursuit of advertising revenue.

This chapter focuses on celebrity porn fakes to explore what they reveal about these intersections between social and synthetic media. In the social media era, more than ever, both celebrity culture and everyday lived experience are about the convergence of the public and the personal. Social media are what connect the celebrity with the fan, the extraordinary with the ordinary, the public with the personal. Public figures use Instagram and TikTok to perform aspects of their everyday and intimate lives, and the everyday and intimate lives of non-famous individuals can also be made public. A site like Pornhub should be understood as social media: its platform architecture; its reliance on users to provide content; its targeted advertising model; its capacity to create a profile and interact with other users; its convergence of public media with personal communication – all are characteristics of social media. Pornhub is a dark reflection of the more celebrated platforms that came to dominate social media by the second decade of the century. This chapter connects deepfake porn videos, by far the largest use of synthetic media to date, to prehistories and precursors, from slash fiction to leaked celebrity sex tapes. And it examines how synthetic porn of ordinary individuals has also begun to emerge, connecting to different currents of involuntary porn.

Ethics and visibility

Porn may be an uncomfortable topic for some readers. So it's important to emphasize that porn is a well-established area of research across the humanities and social sciences, from film studies to criminology. Such attention is drawn by the economics of the porn industries; by the many social and cultural aspects of porn's production, distribution, and consumption; and by its regulatory dimensions. Porn is one cultural space in which societies work out where their limits lie, where they decide what is obscene and what is acceptable (as well as what kinds of obscene are acceptable). This four-letter word at once describes cultural forms, social practices, and business models that bring urgent ethical questions for research about expression and censorship, about sexuality and gender, about identity and technology, about fantasy and desire, about labour and globalization, about health and representation, and about violence, exploitation, and power. J.G. Ballard observed that porn was the most political of genres, because it is about 'how we use and exploit each other in the most urgent and ruthless way' (1984: 98).

What are the ethical dimensions to discussing celebrity deepfake porn videos? The sharing of manipulated and synthetic media demands an ethics of visibility, but so too does their discussion in this kind of book. Digital media research demands that the writer reflect carefully on whom and what they choose to make visible to their readers (Ess 2020; franzke et al. 2020). In initial drafts of

47

the origin of porn

this chapter, I tried to write without using the names or URLs of websites dedicated to celebrity porn deepfakes (referring to them as Site A or Site B, for instance). Because celebrity deepfake porn videos are made without consent, they are a form of abuse, and I was unsure whether it was ethical to point people towards platforms where they can see that abuse for themselves.

But we are not talking here about some hard-to-access underground darknet. The most basic search for the most obvious keywords returns all the largest of these deepfake porn sites within the first few results. Finding these websites is such a trivial thing to do that it feels gestural not to use the sites' names in discussing them. The question was whether making that gesture was the ethical thing to do. Research involves making 'ethically legitimate judgment calls', and uncertainty, ambiguity, and potential disagreement are part of that process (frankze et al. 2020: 6). I concluded that identifying certain websites allows me to properly describe them, and at times quote from and cite them, and that this would in turn let me better communicate the nature and scale of the problems of deepfake porn – because there are most definitely problems, and I do want those problems to be better understood. People who are made the victims of this kind of abuse should have resources that they can draw upon in standing against it. And they should be able to do this in a context of shared understanding of the technological tools that have been used in that abuse.

For this book, I also decided to use the names of celebrities who have been the victims of involuntary porn deepfakes, because otherwise the scope and scale of the issue and what it actually involves would not be clear enough. Just writing 'actor' or 'celebrity' would not properly represent the problem. The women who are most often the subjects of such videos are famous from particular kinds of fantasy film and TV franchises, which is relevant to the discussion. But trying to keep the names at a remove by writing, for instance, '*Game of Thrones* star' or '*Harry Potter* actor' would do nothing to mask their identities, and nor would a further remove such as 'Israeli movie star'.

The need to reflect on and make such choices points to the wider need for an ethics of visibility in relation to networked digital media. Celebrity deepfake porn is in many ways an extreme topic, but the ethical questions it raises go much wider, into many more banal and everyday moments of digital communication. Many of these questions are about mediated visibility: about who and what are made visible to whom; about reflecting critically on what we watch, share, and circulate online; about considering what we tag or copy or link. It's not only digital media researchers, but all digital media users who need to ask themselves these questions. These questions apply much more widely, in many more circumstances of daily digital life, and sometimes an extreme case such as celebrity porn deepfakes is useful to illuminate the existence of these more everyday choices. Such choices become more complex still because of the ways that social media platforms coax their users into ever more disclosure and visibility, because this is the engine of their business models. We are all positioned and pushed to share and forward and retweet everything we see online. But we should all think carefully about why, when, and whether we should.

A brief prehistory of deepfake porn

Deepfakes first appeared as porn. The term *deepfake* itself emerged in 2017 from the name of a forum on the social media platform Reddit; *deepfakes* was also the screen name of the key user of that forum, who created it on 2 November 2017 (Ajder et al. 2019: 3). The members of this now-defunct subreddit were making and sharing synthetic videos in which the likenesses of female celebrities such as Gal Gadot or Taylor Swift were digitally manipulated onto the bodies of performers in actual porn videos (Cole 2017). Reddit has a particular history with non-consensual pornographic imagery (Massanari 2017). It was once the home of popular forums such as /r/creepshots and /r/jailbait, devoted to sharing sexualized images of women that were often taken in public without their knowledge, as in so-called 'upskirting' photos (Chan 2018). Other forms of involuntary porn have included the sharing of intimate photos taken in consensual contexts but then published without the consent of their subjects. Reddit's first deepfakes forum had reached more than 90,000 subscribers in a few weeks before the platform took it down (Kelion 2018). Other online spaces immediately took its place, and there are now many thousands of synthetic celebrity porn videos, with more created every day.

How big an issue is this? In September 2019, synthetic media monitoring company Deeptrace (later renamed Sensity) reported that they had identified almost 15,000 different deepfake videos online. Of those, 96% were said to be fake celebrity porn, and the four major websites for sharing these had combined views of 134 million (Ajder et al. 2019). Content on those deepfake porn websites at that time featured 100% female subjects, whereas deepfakes on other portals such as YouTube, which are generally not porn, featured 61% male subjects. By March 2021, Sensity reported that the number of deepfake videos they could detect online was doubling every six months, with their revised total at that time standing at more than 85,000 videos (Patrini 2021: 2). Globally, around two-thirds of deepfake videos targeted female subjects, with the majority of content in every country being pornographic. Non-consensual deepfake porn, then, is both the predominant use of synthetic video to date, and a phenomenon that so far overwhelmingly targets women.

This is in some ways not surprising. Porn is more central to mediated communication than is often acknowledged. From cave paintings to hook-up apps, people always find ways to use each new medium for sexual representation. Gutenberg may have started by printing the Bible, but new forms of pornography also arrived quickly with the printing press (Eisenstein 1983: 94; Briggs & Burke 2020: 59–61). Within just three years of the invention of photography, an even more significant medium for porn than print, the US Congress had already passed new laws outlawing obscene imagery, as the new medium was immediately applied to the creation of the first nude photos (Sullivan & McKee 2015: 48). Photography was followed by an ever-expanding range of technologies of visibility, all of which found early applications in porn, from cinema to webcams, comics to cable TV, magazines to camcorders (Coopersmith 1998). Even videogames have explored the explicit representation of sex within the constraints of classification and censorship restriction, from the hypersexual representation and 'jiggle physics' applied to female characters and avatars (Brown 2018: 242) to the animated sex scenes hidden in *Grand Theft Auto: San Andreas*. Indie developers use Patreon to fund erotic game releases and sex game platforms such as Nutaku to distribute them, while fan communities develop sexual content in edited versions (mods) of virtual worlds such as Skyrim (Joho 2020).

Porn is significant for media because it is often one of the earliest uses to which a new medium will be put, and so access to porn has driven the commercial adoption of some systems, notably the change in distribution methods made possible by home video in the 1980s:

> [I]n the history of new communication technologies it is clear that demand for, and take-up of, new technologies has been consistently driven by the desire of audiences to access pornographic material more easily and more privately. (Sullivan & McKee 2015: 49)

It's not just that people will turn to a new medium for porn, but that porn can also be a significant factor in how that medium develops. Porn industries and their consumers' demands have at times been drivers of innovations and adaptations (Coopersmith 1998). For example, the use of webcams, now so central to online life, first became prominent through the voyeuristic aspects of turn-of-the-century camgirls such as Jennifer Ringley of Jennicam (Senft 2008). In the case of the early web, porn was a significant engine of developments in payment, video, and advertising technologies, because it was something that people were prepared to pay to access online:

> Safe credit card processing systems, streaming video technologies, hosting services, promotional design practices such as banner advertisements, mouse-trapping, and pop-ups were first developed for and applied on porn sites. (Paasonen 2018a: 551)

So it's not surprising that synthetic media were first deployed in the creation of porn videos. Moreover, it's not surprising that sexual content continues to drive developments in this area, such as the simplification and domestication of synthetic media applications, to which we will turn in the last section of this chapter.

Pornhub is the template for all the dedicated deepfake porn video sites, so it is worth discussing in a bit more detail here to provide some context. These porn sites are very much part of the wider social media ecosystem. Pornhub is itself modelled on YouTube, with a clear echo of that platform's early years, in which communication between video-makers and between viewers was emphasized more through the options to discover content by searching not only for *most viewed*, but also *most favorited*, *most discussed*, and *most responded* (Burgess & Green 2018). Visitors to Pornhub can search videos by multiple categories, including porn genre, performer, most viewed, top rated, playlists, 'popular homemade', 'top earners', and 'viewer's choice', as well as live webcam streams. There is also a 'community' section, which combines DIY, amateur, and pro-am content with messaging, chat, and external links.

Pornhub was founded in 2007, and bought by the porn conglomerate now known as MindGeek three years later. By 2021, the site was claiming 130 million unique visitors every day (Pornhub Insights 2021) and was a major internet presence. In the UK, for example, one-third of all online adults, or 15 million people, visited Pornhub in September 2020, according to media regulator Ofcom (2021: 100). MindGeek's aggressive acquisitions strategy built the firm into one of the world's most significant internet businesses (Paasonen, Jarrett & Light 2019). In part, this was achieved by securing external investment to buy any viable competitors and to buy platforms with complementary services in order to establish a dominant market position: a strategy similar to that which saw Google buy YouTube and Facebook buy WhatsApp and Instagram. Founder Fabian Thylmann described to one interviewer how he first became interested in the commercial possibilities of online porn in the 1990s on Compuserve bulletin boards where people would share passwords to paywalled porn sites, allowing others in the forum to download the content for free (Ronson 2017). This principle of users pooling their access to paid content and then sharing it for free informed the development of Pornhub, and connects to other models of file-sharing and P2P (peer-to-peer) cultures, from the early music earthquake of Napster through warez sites to BitTorrent and on through the music blogs of the 2000s (David 2010; Witt 2015). This model is always that somebody gets the paid content and then shares it with everyone else for free. Thylmann describes Pornhub as modelled specifically on the most obvious social media platform: 'YouTube for porn. So YouTube, just the same logic: videos uploaded by people that are basically porn users. Make money with ads. That's it' (interviewed in Ronson 2017).

Contemporary approaches to filming porn make it well suited to the creation of deepfakes. So-called *gonzo porn* is a bare physical spectacle. Often recorded in the male performer's point-of-view shot on a single hand-held camera, it is porn that dispenses with narrative, character, continuity editing, music, or much of a script (Zecca 2018). Gonzo can be seen as the commercialization of amateur/DIY porn enabled by camcorders (Stella 2016), which can in turn be seen as part of the wider twenty-first-century trend towards media built around the representation and activities of 'ordinary people', from reality TV to talkback radio to social media (Turner 2010). Synthetic porn videos generally draw on such gonzo genres because these are convenient for the limitations of deepfake technologies. Building a synthetic celebrity fake on a gonzo text enables deepfake creators to focus on simply editing the female performer's face without having to follow her through changes of scene, dialogue, or multiple cameras. It would be more technically challenging to sustain a convincing deepfake across a complex narrative with dialogue and multiple camera angles.

The fact that pornographic uses are generally found for every medium makes some people wary of emerging communication technologies. Many media are technologies of visibility, making it possible for us to see and show things that we couldn't before. This often makes people anxious. The anxiety in these cases is not just about a new vector for the distribution of porn, but about a new means of framing and presenting reality. The problem with 'fake' imagery is that it proposes other kinds of imagery as 'real', when in fact they are also mediated, framed, composed, selected. Photographs and videos are both written and read. The history of communication media in western cultures is studded with famous controversies over the dangers of some form of reading or writing: from Exodus and its Ten Commandments' injunctions against making certain kinds of image (Postman & Paglia 2007 [1991]), or Socrates' warnings in Plato's *Phaedrus* about the side-effects of writing, and on through the arrival of print, telegraphy, broadcasting, cinema, recorded music, videogames, and the internet. All of these have been seen by some as enabling particular kinds of dangerous writing and dangerous reading.

This association can fuel moral panics, as new kinds of problem people are identified and said to be using problem technologies. A timeless example is *Time*

55

magazine's notorious 1995 'Cyberporn' cover story (Elmer-DeWitt 1995). The report relied on a crude undergraduate essay as what proved to be worthless evidence for an argument that the nascent internet should be censored. The timing and prominence of the cover story meant that it also served as a first encounter with the very idea of the internet for many of its readers. Some readers might object that I'm doing something similar in this chapter, in connecting emerging synthetic media with porn, and also in taking a normative position that involuntary deepfake porn is a kind of abuse. Is this moral panic material too? To those readers I would respond that I try to avoid writing about this topic in the future tense, and that I try to avoid hypotheticals such as 'the potential' of what 'could happen' with deepfake porn. In this chapter, I'm not writing about what problem people might one day do with problem technologies. I'm writing only about deepfake material that already exists.

MrDeepFakes

MrDeepFakes is the largest and most elaborate of the dedicated celebrity synthetic porn websites. It not only hosts thousands of videos, but also has a large and active community of users who share resources and advice on how to make deepfakes, as well as forums where users submit requests, including paid commissions. So this three-part role as video repository, training resource, and marketplace sets it apart from other sites dedicated to hosting deepfake porn. MrDeepFakes organizes its site and content on the model of Pornhub. As of February 2022, MrDeepFakes claimed more than 275,000 members. This is a striking number in many ways, but there are likely to be many more visitors than that. This is because it is not necessary to create an account in order to watch deepfake porn videos on the site. Even becoming a member involves simply entering any email address, real or false. Having done this, members gain extra levels of site access, including the ability to message other members, to follow individual users who upload particular preferred content, and to curate videos into playlists. But most of the site's content and features are freely available, which implies many more users than those who have bothered to sign up (see Popova 2020 for a different perspective that argues this site works to limit its videos to a particular community).

The site has a list of rules for users, which includes 'be respectful' – a striking stipulation on a site dedicated to non-consensual sexual imagery:

1. You must be 18+ years of age to browse MrDeepFakes. com.
2. No spam. Any automated messages, advertisements or links not related to the discussion will be deleted.
3. Be respectful. Do not troll, attack, or harass other members of the community.
4. All images, videos and discussion of pornography must be only of 18+ models.
5. DO NOT upload or publish content of non-celebrity individuals that would not be considered 'public figures'.
6. DO NOT request fakes of non-celebrities without their consent.
7. ALL new threads and discussions should be primarily in English.

The landing page shows previews of dozens of recently updated videos. The accompanying metadata for each video include technical details about the resolution or the source of the images in the celebrity faceset, and details of the original porn video and performer on whom the fake is based.

MrDeepFakes accepts paid advertising. While it is free to watch any of the videos on the site, and it would also be possible to download a copy of a video without paying, users are invited to pay the creator of a monetized video, and payment may return a link to a higher-resolution download. Payment can be in crypto-currencies or by purchasing tokens. One hundred tokens cost US$1.99 at the time of writing, with a typical video likely to cost 200 or 300 tokens. One prolific creator, who is careful to describe their celebrity abuse videos as 'erotic satire', has uploaded more than 300 videos, and offers a link to their profile on a crowdfunding/patronage website where the user can subscribe to their posts for $15 a month.

For such heavily invested users, MrDeepFakes has a 'Creators Program', which again is visibly inspired by Pornhub's revenue-sharing ventures such as its 'Model Program' or its 'Content Partner Program'. These in turn draw upon YouTube's history of partnership ventures to develop content creators who will drive traffic to the platform. MrDeepFakes offers verified uploaders the options to monetize their content: they can choose to charge for downloads or to add a suggested donation button to their videos. In the same way that YouTube's development of its various partnership and creators programmes has worked to mutually foster and reinforce the connection and benefits of being on YouTube for both the individual uploader and the platform, the MrDeepFakes programme works to try to deeper embed active uploaders within the site's user and advertising ecology. This is a branding strategy to try to ensure the site's future development.

As well as videos, MrDeepFakes hosts a forum area that is divided into sections. There are announcements and there is news. There are listings of celebrity deepfake videos, there is a section for requests, including a separate section for paid commissions, and there are similar sections for synthetic photos. There is a smaller section for non-pornographic content and requests; plus there are areas for general discussion and suggestions, and to claim credit for videos or to flag them. The heart of these forums is the 'DeepFake Creation Tools' area for advice on how to create synthetic videos. The site hosts extensive training materials on how to use DeepFaceLab 2.0, a face-swapping system used by many of the most prominent creators of synthetic media. The site walks the user through how to extract images of their chosen celebrity from an existing video and how to edit and prepare these into a faceset for the machine-learning networks. It explains how to optimize and align images between the source and target videos, how to train the neural networks, how to merge the resulting images, and how to use basic post-production techniques to refine the final synthetic product.

By far the biggest section is that for 'Questions', which as of February 2022 included more than 2,300 threads with a total of more than 10,800 posts. This is considerably larger than any of the other sections, even those requesting videos of particular celebrities. These 2,300+ 'Questions' threads are about technical aspects of how to create synthetic porn videos. This is more than three times larger than the next largest section, which is itself about a specific technical aspect of creating deepfakes: making, finding, and sharing celebrity image facesets. The section with the next largest overall number of posts is the general 'Guides and Tutorials' section.

The numbers are far higher than those requesting, commissioning, or posting actual videos.

So MrDeepFakes is not just a place where people view such videos. It is a place dedicated to making them. It is a site of *participatory culture* (Jenkins 2008; Delwiche & Henderson 2013). It has been clear for some years that the redistribution of access to media space that has been made possible by networked digital media is not necessarily democratic or progressive. Media scholars in the internet era, myself included, have often written as though opening up more spaces for more voices would necessarily be a good thing. But it's clear that some of those voices will also be repressive, harassing, exploitative, misogynistic, or abusive. The 'people formerly known as the audience' (Rosen 2006) are not only interested in adding constructive perspectives to the news or taking part in TikTok dance challenges. Some of them are interested in commissioning non-consensual pornography and soliciting machine-learning advice from others more expert in the software than they are. And this too is participatory culture.

Celebrity skin

As with Pornhub, the navigation options on the site are visibly influenced by early YouTube and by the ecology of porn tube sites that it inspired. Here again users can navigate through the thousands of videos on the site through a range of metrics and categories: latest videos, most viewed and top rated, and also by porn genre or keyword. Suggested keywords at the foot of each page list various generic sex acts as well as some more specific to deepfakes, including *K-Pop, Bollywood, YouTuber, Twitch,* and *Emma Watson.* There are almost 500 synthetic videos of Emma Watson on this website alone, enough to make that essentially a separate porn genre on its own. There are extensive curated collections of the particular celebrities featured in the videos and also separate curated pages of the porn performers whose bodies are used in the clips.

In the cases of certain prominent women actors from popular sci-fi and fantasy franchises, there are hundreds of different fake porn videos of each. Online fan cultures are often celebrated for their enabling of progressive activist fandoms (Jenkins 2008; Jenkins, Ito & boyd 2016), but these deepfakes demonstrate a particular kind of toxic fandom. By *toxic*, I mean fan behaviours that assert ownership over their favourite shows, films, or performers. Social media enable this through their convergence of public and personal communication. We can perform our tastes for large communities of others who share them. These may be anonymous, like 4Chan, or pseudonymous, like much of Reddit or Twitter. Provocative or outrageous posts can be rewarded with attention and status within a community (Massanari 2017). At scale, fandoms can threaten to take hostages and make demands. *Star Wars* fans hounded Vietnamese-American actor Kelly Marie Tran off social media in their bullying responses to her part in *The Last Jedi*. DC fans campaigned for an alternative version of a Justice League movie through the hashtag #ReleaseTheSnyderCut. Almost 2 million *Game of Thrones* fans signed a petition at Change.org to have its final season remade 'with competent writers'.

Such toxic fandom is about seeing an artist as one's personal property. And this mindset drives celebrity deepfake porn, through which the actual faces and bodies of stars are claimed, appropriated, and manipulated. The women whose likenesses are most often made to appear in these videos are from particular kinds of fantasy film and TV shows that generate large and passionate fandoms. There are also large numbers of deepfake porn videos of Bollywood stars and of K-Pop performers. I found very few synthetic porn videos of male celebrities in researching this chapter. Those I did find all featured Marvel actors – Chris Evans, Chris Pratt, Tom Holland – with the exception of a single video each of Justin Bieber and of UK royal Prince Harry.

Prominent celebrities are ranked on MrDeepFakes by the number of synthetic porn videos of them available. This metric of 'most videos' establishes and promotes a certain hierarchy, and a certain way of reading the site. The list of names tells a particular story, with the majority of the top twenty being stars of major fantasy franchises. It also reinforces it, as creators are able to see where demand lies and what the community values. This reading is the one dominated by Marvel and DC, by *Harry Potter* and *Star Wars*, joined in this list by two of the biggest pop stars in the English-speaking world, four K-Pop performers, and one Twitch streamer. As of February 2022, there were twenty-four women who had been the victims of more than a hundred videos each on this single website alone. According to the site's own public metrics at that date, the celebrities who have been the subjects of the largest numbers of videos on MrDeepFakes are as shown in Table 1.

Each curated page for a particular celebrity has its own accompanying text at the foot of the page, and these texts convey a great deal about the nature and tone of the site. The Emma Watson page, for example, carries the following text:

MrDeepFakes has the best Emma Watson deepfake porn videos and fake Emma Watson nude photos. So

Table 1. Celebrities who have most often been the subject in MrDeepFakes videos as of February 2022

Target	Number of videos
Emma Watson	478
Scarlett Johansson	410
Gal Gadot	309
Natalie Portman	277
Margot Robbie	277
Daisy Ridley	236
Taylor Swift	214
Ariana Grande	211
Angelina Jolie	186
IU	172
Chloë Grace Moretz	163
Elizabeth Olsen	163
Jennie	159
Jennifer Lawrence	153
Emilia Clarke	151
Pokimane	136
Irene	127
Satomi Ishihara	119
Jessica Alba	116
Brie Larson	114

Source: Created by the author. Data gathered from www.mrdeepfakes.com.

you came looking for Emma Watson dirty videos and Emma Watson topless photos? Looks like you've hit the jackpot! With the latest AI technology, users can create convincing Emma Watson sextapes and even remove clothes to create Emma Watson nude photos. Here you will find all the fapping material you need from Emma Watson stripping naked, to giving blowjobs, handjobs,

63

taking anal, sexy feet and much more! There's nothing better than viewing sexy Emma Watson fullfilling [*sic*] your perverted dreams in a realistic fake.

Many of these videos present as being films of the fictional characters played by these women on screen, rather than of the actors themselves: they are described to the user as Wonder Woman porn, not Gal Gadot abuse; as Harley Quinn porn, not Margot Robbie abuse. This connects with decades of slash fiction, in which fans of particular characters write and share erotic stories about those characters, and the comparison is worth exploring further. The archetypal slash case has always been Kirk and Spock from *Star Trek*, with the abbreviation Kirk/Spock becoming K/S, and the slash between their initials providing the name of the genre. Slash has variously been understood as assertions of female sexual agency, as political engagements with gay representations in the media, and as explorations of queer representations (Penley 1991; Busse & Lothian 2018; Popova 2020).

Slash fictions are a way of reading a film or a show but are also, and above all, a way of *writing* it. You might watch a particular Marvel film and then imagine yourself having sex with the character Black Widow or Captain America, or their actor Scarlett Johansson or Chris Evans. You might use visual aids from the film or its marketing to fuel that fantasy. But the fantasy remains in your imagination. The fantasy is a way of *reading* the film, and of reading both its characters and the celebrities who perform them. Slash describes one way that you might also *write* that fantasy. You might try to represent the fantasy to yourself or to others by writing erotic fan fiction about it (Vermorel 1985). Much of the history of such fiction is about fantasizing relationships between the *characters* performed: that archetypal slash genre is called K/S for Kirk/Spock, not S/N for Shatner/Nimoy (although real-person slash does exist, for example, about members of BTS or One Direction). You might also invite the reader into this fantasy by writing a Y/N fiction, in which Y/N stands for Your/Name and the reader is to substitute their own name in the text as that character's encounters with, say, Hermione or Draco develop. This is again the convergence of the personal and the public that characterizes the contemporary digital media environment.

If we use *writing* more broadly to include creating images, such as synthetic porn videos, then the differences between this and slash start to become clearer. To appropriate the faces of Natalie Portman or Scarlett Johansson and manipulate those into an actual hardcore porn video is to *write* a new part for those performers to play and to actually *produce and exhibit* it on video. A synthetic Marvel porn video that features the faces of those actual actors is a very different thing from a prose story about those characters. It is not just reading the characters as a fantasy, but writing the faces of real people into that fantasy and then publishing it to unknowable audiences. This is not transgressive or edgy, it is misogynistic and abusive.

Why is this? It's important to see deepfake porn within a much wider pattern of abusive online misogyny: as part of the same spectrum as upskirting, doxxing, unsolicited dick pics, identity theft, stalking, and myriad other forms of harassment of women online. Deepfakes also, as Emily van der Nagel argues, 'continue a long history of women's images being used to harass, humiliate, and harm them' (2020: 424). Emma Jane's important work on online misogyny argues that the contemporary proliferation of gendered cyberhate is best understood as emerging from a combination of new technologies, subcultural capital and appropriation, individual psychologies, mob dynamics, and, most importantly, systemic gender inequity (including a backlash against feminist gains and activism). Misogynists have never had so many opportunities to collectivise and abuse women with so few consequences. Female targets have never been so visible and instantly accessible in such large numbers. (2017: 51)

So synthetic media are part of a proliferation of new means of digital harassment in the twenty-first century networked environment. Networked digital media make such misogyny more visible, but they also increase opportunities for such abuse. They can even enable abusers to feel part of a community, as the convergence of public and personal communication can confer status on those who are most effective at publicizing their personal views, however repellent those views can seem to people outside their group.

Hard truths

Fantasy and reality may be too hard to separate when it comes to sexual desire. The reality of sex is informed by fantasy, and such fantasy draws on experiences of reality (or on a lack of these). Things get significantly more complicated when the fantasy involves celebrities who are associated with particular fictional characters, because their celebrity image is itself the product of several layers of fantasy, and so is the fictional character they portray. It's not just the *faces* of celebrities that are taken in this way, but their star images too. Gal Gadot is used in deepfake videos not just because of her physical attributes, but also because of her cultural position within a certain kind of screen franchise. Those videos present the character of Wonder Woman in sexual content as much as they present Gadot – perhaps more so. This is not a justification for such content (I'm not going to offer any justifications for it). Instead, it is an observation about the different levels of meaning that are being manipulated in such videos.

First, there are the meanings around the first individual, non-consenting person (Gal Gadot), whose face is manipulated into an existing pornographic video. How much can she control the uses of *images* of her face produced in Hollywood films and promotional material? Celebrity and sexual representation have always intersected in complex ways, with the star images of some celebrities coming to represent prevailing or changing social and cultural attitudes towards sex and sexuality (Dyer 2004; Evans 2018). There have always been celebrities who make themselves visible in more or less pornographic ways, from Marilyn Monroe's appearance as the nude centrefold in the first issue of *Playboy* to the career-moves of deliberately leaked home sex tapes (Hayward & Rahn 2015; Longstaff 2018) or sexualized performances in night-vision sequences on reality TV (Kavka 2018). The digital media era has also seen celebrities made visible by others in non-consensual ways, from stolen home sex tapes to the mass hack of iCloud accounts in 2014, when scores of female celebrities, including Jennifer Lawrence, Rihanna, and Scarlett Johansson, had their personal nude photos posted online (Meikle 2016: 102–6). Websites such as Celeb Jihad aggregate such images alongside deepfakes and authentic nude appearances from non-porn films, accompanying them with aggressive and abusive commentaries. The convergence of public and personal that characterizes social media has also brought a blurring of categories such as *amateur* and *professional* porn (Paasonen 2018b).

Second, there are the meanings around the other individual, non-consenting people in the video, the porn performers whose bodies are also appropriated for the deepfake. We can be certain that Gadot has not consented to her use in these videos, but we should not forget that the performers whose bodies are used here have not given consent for this manipulation of their appearance either. There is a sense in which these performers are being erased, their sexual labour being further devalued by their replacement with the face of a celebrity, with someone who is seen to *matter*. Indeed, this lack of consent from the porn performer can be true not just of the deepfake but perhaps of the original porn content too. In emphasizing the non-consensual aspects of deepfake porn, it would be wrong to draw too strong a contrast and assume that all other porn is consensual in some simple way. Heather Berg's 2021 ethnographic study of porn performers shows the complexities of distinguishing between consent and desire, and the different kinds of calculus of consent that inform decisions about what people will and will not agree to do on camera for money.

Much porn, perhaps most, may be consensual representation of adult sex, but there are clear currents of criminality and abuse too. There is, for example, an entire genre of amateur casting videos, in which the performer plays the part of a newcomer on camera for the first time. Some of these productions may be of professionals acting a part, but others have featured genuine amateurs whose participation involved deception and coercion. A company called 'Girls Do Porn' was successfully sued by twenty-two women who had been deceived and coerced into having sex in its 'casting couch' videos (Levensen 2020). Girls Do Porn was promoted by Pornhub as premium material, and its channel had received more than 670 million views by the time of its removal in 2020 (Cole 2019a). More than forty women subsequently sued Pornhub and MindGeek, alleging that the firm had profited from sex trafficking by the Girls Do Porn owners and had failed to remove videos in which they appeared despite multiple takedown notices and evidence of criminality as early as 2009 (BBC News 2020a). Images from Girls Do Porn and Czech Casting, a similar audition-themed porn site that has been accused of coercion, rape, and human trafficking, have been used in datasets to train neural networks to generate synthetic porn images (Cole, Maiberg & Koslerova 2020). To use the actual sexual abuse of real individual women as raw material for software development is to make that abuse into a kind of template. It's a template in which questions of sexual consent have been completely abandoned, and – central to the argument of this book – questions of consent to the use of one's digital data have too.

And third, by a long distance, there are the meanings around the DC comics franchise of Wonder Woman, which motivates the choice of Gadot for the deepfake. Fandoms remix and reuse their favourite stories and images in all kinds of ways, sometimes subverting the industry that produces these, sometimes fuelling it (Jenkins 2008). To some fans, a Wonder Woman porn video may appear part of a continuum with fan art, fan fiction, or other fan videos about the character. DC are not the only ones who get to tell Wonder Woman stories, as questions of intellectual property encounter the sheer cultural ubiquity of successful franchise characters. The face in the video for some viewers may be less that of Gadot than that of Wonder Woman. Here the problem gets caught up with questions of the manufacture of celebrity and the industrial production of star images. I have little concern for DC, whose business is more than big enough to survive fan content. But it is true that there are copyright dimensions to the deepfake content as well, however secondary those are to the other levels of consent here.

As well as viewing MrDeepFakes's 'most videos' section, the user can also navigate the site by browsing the most-viewed videos. There is the option to view these in four periods: *All Time*, *This Month*, *This Week*, *Today*. These are not just different ways to explore the same content, but lead to quite different results. These ways of reading the site tell different stories, although not better ones. There are seventeen different women featured in the twenty most-viewed individual videos, each of which has been watched more than a million times. Thirteen of these women are prominent in the Indian entertainment industries, along with three American TikTok personalities and one American performer most associated with Marvel films. As of February 2022, the women used in the site's twenty all-time most-viewed videos were as shown in Table 2.

So while the women with the most different videos made of them are mainly from Hollywood, the subjects of the most-viewed videos are concentrated around Bollywood. The problems of synthetic celebrity porn, then, have global variants. It's not a problem confined to a particular part of the world. Sensity reported in 2021 that, in some territories, including China, India,

70

Table 2. The twenty all-time most-viewed videos on
MrDeepFakes as of February 2022

Target	Number of views
Tamanna Bhatia	4,721,977
Aishwarya Rai	4,112,157
Shraddha Kapoor	3,238,464
Rashmika Mandanna	2,422,531
Tamanna Bhatia	2,373,974
Jacqueline Fernandez	1,857,577
Bella Poarch	1,821,676
Addison Rae	1,719,684
Samantha Akkineni	1,718,100
Dixie D'Amelio	1,677,528
Sonakshi Sinha	1,642,513
Trisha Krishnan	1,608,616
Elizabeth Olsen	1,525,643
Aishwarya Rai	1,468,908
Keerthy Suresh	1,417,934
Urvashi Rautela	1,375,872
Kareena Kapoor	1,372,188
Sara Ali Khan	1,368,589
Anupama Parameswaran	1,366,280
Shraddha Kapoor	1,255,171

Source: Created by the author. Data gathered from www.
mrdeepfakes.com.

Japan, and South Korea, more than 90% of synthetic
videos were of women, the majority in each case
being pornographic (Patrini 2021: 4). Future deepfake
research will no doubt explore how these technologies
are localized in specific cultural contexts (see de Seta
2021 for one such discussion of Chinese *huanlian* or
face-swapping content).

Domesticating deepfake abuse

Synthetic media porn is being domesticated. It is not just a phenomenon that affects the famous. Users can now employ a range of tools to create synthetic sexual content of their own, including generating non-consensual imagery of ordinary people whom they know. As part of its guides and tutorials sections, MrDeepFakes hosts advice on how to find a porn performer who is a physical match for the desired subject. It links to a dedicated facial recognition website called Porn Star by Face. This site describes itself as 'The First Porn Star face-recognizing search engine based on deep neural networks', although there are also similar tools such as Find Porn Face. The idea is that the user can find porn videos featuring performers who resemble someone they know and would like to see in a porn video. For creators, it also allows them to identify a likely source video for use with their target subject. The user can drag-and-drop an image of their chosen person (the site so far only works with women), and the site's neural networks create a pattern of the face, mapping key features such as eyebrows, lips, and nose shapes, and comparing those with its database of mapped porn performers to suggest possible matches. 'The neural network is trained with every request you make,' says the site, 'so please share the link with your friends.'

It is not obvious what happens to the images once they have been added to this database: while the site states that it doesn't store uploaded photos, it also posts a log of how many women are in its database (almost 4,000 as of February 2022) and there is no way for the user to be sure that a photo they upload will not be used for any other purpose, or to be confident in the site's security. This is important, because it should be obvious that the user can add a photo of anyone they know, not just a celebrity. The site in fact nudges the user in the direction of uploading non-celebrities with a wink emoticon:

Step 1. Upload a photo of an actress or girl you know ;)
Step 2. The system detects the face.
Step 3. Enjoy the result!

Deepfake pornography is not something that only happens to superstar actors. Ordinary people can also be the targets.

A crucial example of this is the case of DeepNude. This was originally a Windows and Linux app launched on 23 June 2019. The app invited users to upload a photo of a woman and within thirty seconds the app would generate a version of the image in which she was naked. The free image would be obscured by a watermark that could be removed if the user paid US$50 for the app's premium version (Ajder et al. 2019: 8). The logo was a retro cartoon image referencing x-ray glasses, with the slogan 'The superpower you always wanted'. After journalist Samantha Cole (2019b) wrote about DeepNude ('This horrifying app undresses a photo of any woman with a single click'), the site was slammed with more than half a million download requests. Overwhelmed, the site's operators took the app offline, releasing a statement on Twitter just four days after their launch:

Despite the safety measures adopted (watermarks) if 500,000 people use it, the probability that people will misuse it is too high. We don't want to make money this way. Surely some copies of DeepNude will be shared on the web, but we don't want to be the ones who sell it. The world is not yet ready for DeepNude. (Posted by @ deepnudeapp, 27 June 2019)

One wonders what kinds of uses might be implied to contrast with 'misuse' here, and what might constitute the world being 'ready for DeepNude'. But ready or not, and despite the promise not to sell copies of the app, its creators did sell its code for $US30,000 on 19 July 2019, and versions of the code now circulate widely online (Ajder et al. 2019: 8).

Why does this matter? First, it shows very clearly the gendered power relationships that characterize this kind of software. DeepNude is only able to generate naked images of women. Images of men don't work. This is because the neural networks powering DeepNude were trained on a database of 10,000 images of naked women – no men (Cole 2019b). This technology is not neutral (they never are), but one that comes with its own inbuilt politics. It both embodies and expresses particular kinds of gendered power relations. The selection of the data and images used in training the DeepNude model is a stark example of how algorithmic media can reinforce existing social problems.

The second reason this case matters is that it is an important part of the domestication of synthetic media applications designed for sexual uses and abuses. Versions of the DeepNude software quickly became available as websites, so that involuntary nudes can be generated by uploading to the browser rather than having to install any software. This removes most technical barriers to use, and makes it as simple as uploading a photo to Facebook. Such uses of synthetic media and visualization technologies are already within the reach of the most technologically clueless of users.

Sensity reported in 2020 that an automated version of the DeepNude code was being used to run a bot within the messaging app Telegram (Ajder, Patrini & Cavalli 2020). This version ran on smartphones, marking a further level of simplification and domestication of the technology. Sensity identified a network of channels within Telegram with a combined population of more than 100,000 users, mostly from Russia and neighbouring countries, despite Telegram being banned in Russia at the time. The Russian social media platform VK had bought substantial advertising in the channels and the bot was widely discussed on hundreds of pages on that platform. As of July 2020, Sensity calculated that 104,852 women had been the victims of DeepNude-style attacks using the Telegram bot and had had their synthetic images shared within the wider networks; the report assumed that many others had also been targeted privately, with the resulting image kept private by the individual user rather than shared in Telegram channels.

Another significant site for such activity is DeepSukebe, which describes itself as 'an AI-leveraged nudifier'. DeepSukebe drew significant traffic throughout 2021, in part through referrals in the MrDeepFakes user forums. As with DeepNude, this site allows the user to upload a photo of any woman and receive a synthetic nude version. The BBC reported the site had more than 5 million visits in June 2021 alone (Wakefield 2021). While some features of DeepSukebe can be used for free, it offers higher-quality and unlimited images to users with a paid subscription. Users referring the site to others get credit if their friends sign up, driving expansion and visibility for DeepSukebe. In common with other such projects, DeepSukebe adds high-minded claims to its low-minded offer: its home page says the site is about 'Revealing truth hidden under clothing' and declares that 'At last, the dream that humans have long desired came true'. It has a logo with the legend 'We seek truth / We strip fakes / We deny lies'. But behind this rhetoric, its business is enabling the creation of abusive sexual images of women.

The personal consequences for the victims of such abuse can be far-reaching. Indian investigative journalist Rana Ayyub was the victim of a synthetic porn video that she believes was intended to undermine her political writing and journalistic reputation. After speaking publicly about a sex scandal linked to the nationalist BJP party, images from Ayyub's Twitter profile began to be manipulated in a targeted disinformation campaign (Ayyub 2018a, 2018b). Then in April 2018, she learned that a synthetic porn video with her face swapped into it was circulating through Indian political groups on WhatsApp. Ayyub's account of what happened next is a chilling insight into the impacts on the victims of this kind of abuse:

> Before I could even gather myself, my phone started beeping and I saw I had more than 100 Twitter notifications, all sharing the video. My friend told me to delete Twitter but I couldn't, I didn't want people to think this was actually me. I went on Facebook and I had been inundated with messages there too. They were trying to derail me, every other person was harassing me with comments like 'I never knew you had such a stunning body'. I deleted my Facebook, I just couldn't take it. But on Instagram, under every single one of my posts, the comments were filling with screenshots of the video. Then, the fanpage of the BJP's leader shared the video and the whole thing snowballed. The video was shared 40,000 more times. It ended up on almost every phone in India. (Ayyub 2018a)

The sexual abuse imagery led to Ayyub being publicly shamed and persecuted at a national level, and to her hospitalization with the effects of the stress. She reports struggling to get police to record her complaint, and that the United Nations eventually intervened to demand the Indian government protect her.

As a prominent journalist writing about controversial topics, Ayyub had something of a public profile. But it's important to recognize that such assaults can also affect random, ordinary individuals with no public profiles at all. As a law student in Australia, Noelle Martin googled herself one day to discover that harmless selfies she had posted online had been copied and manipulated into countless pornographic contexts. The more she tried to have images removed from websites, the more new ones appeared. Some people added Martin's friends on social media platforms in order to get access to new pictures of her (Martin 2017). The abuse escalated from Photoshopped images to deepfake video. The ordeal continued for years, and saw Martin become an activist and victims' advocate as Australian states moved to criminalize such image-based sexual abuse (McGlynn & Rackley 2017).

Noelle Martin's experiences underline that it's not only celebrities who are vulnerable to this kind of predatory activity. And they also illuminate some of the most fundamental characteristics of social media, and the difficulties those characteristics pose for victims of synthetic porn. Once an image or a video is online, it is persistent, searchable, replicable, and scalable (boyd 2011: 46–8). Traces of even the most ephemeral of online moments are recorded and persist as copies pass across networks. Each online interaction becomes part of networked databases that others can search. Computer networks can be understood as copying machines, reproducing images as part of their operations – and so can many people online, who routinely download and save things that they like. Anything online also has the potential to be scaled up to larger, unknown audiences, who may respond in harmful ways.

Synthetic porn technology continues to develop towards simplifying and domesticating deepfake abuse. A website called Yapty, no longer active at the time of writing, allowed users to generate rudimentary deepfake porn by simply uploading a *single photo* of their target and then choosing its destination from a gallery of existing porn videos. The user could choose to view a free preview of the results or pay to download a full-length version of the video. There was no need to get involved in any machine learning or programming, just to post one photo. 'Anyone can be a porn star' read the text on the site's landing page. 'Swap your face with adult models.' There was an upload button and four 'example faces': two male, two female, all perhaps synthetic. The wording was careful to pretend distance from involuntary porn: *swap your face*, not the face of that other person you like. And the site's terms warned the user that 'You must have consent of person(s) that appear in images you upload to the platform'. But this was a flimsy and transparent legal hedge, likely to fool no one. The clear direction of the whole project was towards the creation of non-consensual sexual images of others, while claiming at the same time to be the leading edge of responsible use of synthetic media technology:

> Our deepfake tech lets you experience pornography in a whole new way. Giving us a unique opportunity to make things safer for workers in the industry, and more enjoyable and personal for the curious guys n' gals out

there who want to explore their fantasies. There are a lot of challenges that society has to face up to with deepfake technology, and we're leading the charge to make sure the tech is used responsibly. This is just the beginning. We're building a future where anyone can live out any of their dreams and fantasies.

The site's creator was periodically active in the MrDeepFakes forum from the launch of Yapty in September 2019, and other members were active in sharing examples of what Yapty could do, in giving feedback, and in requesting new features. The examples shared in that forum were all visually very crude and unconvincing, and the dominant notes in the chat threads were disappointment and frustration. A single photo is not much data with which to create a persuasive video. But as with DeepNude, the very real importance of this example is that it is proof-of-concept for this kind of consumer-level deepfake porn creation, and for the extension of this beyond celebrities and into everyday life.

Summary

This chapter has traced the emergence and expansion of synthetic porn, which remains for now by far the biggest category of deepfakes. I set such non-consensual sexual imagery within broader contexts of other porno-graphic media, both consensual and involuntary, and presented research on one key forum to indicate the scope and scale of the problems, as well as debating the ethics of this kind of research. Demand for porn has in the past helped to shape the development of some media technologies, and this is visibly happening with synthetic media, as users explore new ways to simplify and domesticate the creation of deepfake porn: being used as raw material for involuntary sexual imagery is no longer something that only affects famous actors or singers. I have argued in this chapter that such non-consensual synthetic imagery is a logical outcome of the digital media environment in which all lived human experience is reduced to data to be taken, manipulated, and exploited.

3

Remix Aesthetics and Synthetic Media

Marcel Duchamp saw more acutely than most people. Here he is, interviewed about his art for NBC television in 1956: 'Data is the ultimate readymade. Endless copies, perfectly generated in an instant, as if by magic. Humankind stripped bare by its mechanical bachelor. This is the essence of the dataist approach.' To talk about data in artistic terms seems very prescient, even for Duchamp. But it is of course a synthetic video (Posters & Howe 2019a), in which Duchamp's facial features and the movements of his mouth from that grainy black-and-white film (Graff 1956) are remixed to match with the new script, playfully juxtaposing *data* with *Dada*.

The Duchamp deepfake was created by artists Bill Posters and Daniel Howe. In 2019, Posters and Howe collaborated on a deepfake project for Instagram called 'Big Dada/Public Faces', which established them as leading exponents of synthetic media art. This project was a series of short synthetic videos of prominent cultural figures, also exhibited as part of a larger installation called 'Spectre' at the Sheffield Doc/Fest documentary film festival. The artists posted six clips on Posters' Instagram: synthetic videos of Kim Kardashian,

Donald Trump, Mark Zuckerberg, Morgan Freeman, and artists Marina Abramović and Duchamp (Posters & Howe 2019b). In most, the figure talks directly to the camera, with some in close-up, the movements of their facial features accurately matching the spoken words that they have never actually said in real life. The script for the Kardashian monologue gives a good sense of the tone of the project: 'When there's so many haters, I really don't care, because their data has made me rich beyond my wildest dreams. [...] I feel really blessed because I genuinely love the process of manipulating people online for money.'

In a public talk at the Aesthetica Art Prize 'Future Now' Symposium in May 2021, Posters explained how Instagram was chosen as the venue for this art project because of the platform's very lack of a synthetic media policy. Facebook, which owns Instagram, had allowed the repeated sharing of the doctored Nancy Pelosi video discussed in Chapter 1, and so this offered the opportunity for a tactical media response. Uploading a synthetic Mark Zuckerberg video to one of his own platforms was both a provocation and a test.

In naming this deepfakes project 'Big Dada', and in the selection of Duchamp, the artists make a particular kind of claim about their own artistic context and lineage. The deepfake video of Duchamp being inter-viewed identifies connections between his Dadaist emphasis on appropriating images and meanings and our contemporary digital media environment in which all human experience is taken as data by the imperial powers of Google and Amazon, Tencent and Facebook. This chapter pursues some connections and resonances between the remix creativity and creative legacies of Dada and the deepfake appropriations of synthetic media. The term *deepfake* is in some ways a problem because it centres on certain kinds of uses of the technology and closes off others. When we use the term *fake*, we exclude legitimate uses, and point towards the propagandistic and the pornographic. This chapter explores more legitimate uses of synthetic media in creative and artistic contexts.

Unlimited Dada

There were lots of Dadas. There still are. The cacophonous provocations of the Cabaret Voltaire in Zurich were very different from the icy photomontages of Dada in Berlin. The conceptual gestures of New York Dada were not the same as the literary experiments of Paris Dada (Gale 1997; Kuenzli 2006). 'Dada', observed Tristan Tzara, 'is a state of mind' (quoted in Rasula 2015: 246). Each version of Dada was a very specific response to its historical moment, its political climate, and its artistic currents, to the horrors of the First World War and to the creative advances of early modernisms (Bigsby 1972). But in many ways, those different Dadas are all still around, as their influence gets remixed into new contexts. One thing those Dadas all shared was the desire to provoke: for its own sake, as an artistic gesture, as a way to force their audience to see something anew. Another thing they all shared was an approach to creating with found materials that we can now think of as a *remix* aesthetic. Editing texts and editing contexts. André Breton (quoted in Kuenzli 2006: 33) described such Dada tactics as 'the marvellous faculty of attaining two widely separate realities without departing from the realm of our experience, of bringing them together and drawing a spark from their contact' (it took a Surrealist to really get Dada).

83

Duchamp turned the act of selection into a principal artistic technique. In exhibiting a bicycle wheel or a snow shovel in a gallery, what came to count was that the artist had selected the object, not created it (Duchamp 1973). This act of selection made new meanings possible: the bicycle wheel meant something different in a gallery than it did on a bike, and the gallery meant something different once it had a bicycle wheel in it. This was a remix gesture: opening up new meanings by moving things from one context to another. Some of Duchamp's other work achieves its effects by remixing a text or image itself, such as his defaced 'Mona Lisa'. These ideas of remix – of editing a text or image, or of combining existing materials in new contexts – animated much twentieth-century art and culture. All kinds of artists remixed texts or remixed contexts, from magical realist literature to cinematic editing, from jazz built on collaborative improvisation to electronic music built on digital sampling. After Dada, the remix idea was itself remixed from one context to another, through Surrealism, the Situationists, Pop Art, and Appropriation Art. The logic of *cut*, *copy*, and *paste* later converged with digital computing, becoming some of the most basic commands and gestures in everyday media use (Manovich 2013).

In the twenty-first century, social media have taken this in new directions, helping to create the conditions for the emergence of deepfakes. Now we all remix texts and contexts every day. We find or make images and videos and we share them in the new contexts of our profiles and timelines, making possible new meanings for both those images and those profiles. There are echoes in our daily Twitter and Instagram timelines of Tristan Tzara's 1920 algorithm for creating a Dadaist poem:

84

Take a newspaper.

Take some scissors.

Choose from this paper an article of the length you
    want to make your poem.

Cut out the article.

Next carefully cut out each of the words that makes up
    this article and put them all in a bag.

Shake gently.

Next take out each cutting one after the other.

Copy conscientiously in the order in which they left the
    bag.

The poem will resemble you. (Quoted in Gale 1997:
    63–4)

Those timelines filled with our fragments and likes and
shares can be seen as a twenty-first-century expression
of Tzara's idea that we can use found materials and
random combination to create something that resembles
us, that expresses who we are.

The 'Big Dada/Public Faces' deepfakes project reaches
back to those modernist currents when it claims the
moving image of Duchamp himself as raw artistic
material. It remixes this 1950s clip of Duchamp and
sets it in the new context of Instagram to suggest new
meanings around data, power, technology, and control.
Posters and Howe simultaneously appropriate people's
data *and* use this to critique the appropriation of
people's data. So the artistic intent is a different kind of
ironic impulse from that of the celebrity porn videos we
discussed in Chapter 2. Or is it? After all, those porn
videos also appropriate the public faces and star images,
the celebrity meanings, of the famous. A synthetic video
objectifying Scarlett Johansson so that she appears to
be doing porn and a synthetic video representing Mark
Zuckerberg so that he appears to be gloating about the

data economy both claim their available personal data and facial likenesses as fair game. To appropriate an image of the powerful in order to turn that symbol of their power into a question mark is an established artistic gesture. Appropriation of images is a central engine of satire in the digital media age (Ajder & Glick 2021).

But at what point does appropriation become abuse? The answer depends on the power relations. The satirist challenging Mark Zuckerberg on Instagram is less powerful in that relationship than is the Facebook CEO. In the case of Posters and Howe uploading their Zuckerberg deepfake to Instagram, Zuckerberg could have personally ordered the video to be vaporized from the platform. But the toxic fan deciding to cast Scarlett Johansson in a non-consensual porn video has more power in that context than the movie star, who is unable to do much about it. In an interview with the *Washington Post*, Johansson reflected on many failed attempts to block the appropriation of her image, including for stolen nudes, non-consensual porn, and the unauthorized use of her likeness as the face of a life-size robot girlfriend by a Hong Kong designer: 'The fact is that trying to protect yourself from the internet and its depravity is basically a lost cause', Johansson said. 'The internet is a vast wormhole of darkness' (quoted in Harwell 2018b). Appropriating found material for creative or satirical cultural production, whether a bicycle wheel or Mark Zuckerberg's face, is now a very established and legitimate repertoire (Evans 2009). But appropriating Scarlett Johansson's face as material for involuntary pornography is a form of abuse. In these contexts, Mark Zuckerberg can perhaps look after himself, but Scarlett Johansson shouldn't have to. And as we saw in Chapter 2, such abuse is no longer directed only at the famous.

What you are about to see is not real

Posters and Howe's Zuckerberg video has him seated at a desk talking to camera, and is overlaid with CBS chyrons that make it resemble a clip from its online CBSN streaming news channel. 'Imagine this for a second,' Zuckerberg is made to say. 'One man with total control of billions of people's stolen data. All their secrets, their lives, their futures. [...] Whoever controls the data controls the future.' Soon after its release in June 2019, reporters for the *Washington Post* (Chiu 2019) and for *Vice* (Cole 2019c) picked up on this video and its connection to the Pelosi case, and their coverage triggered a wave of stories in international media: in the *New York Times*, *Le Monde*, *La Repubblica*, *Süddeutsche Zeitung*, and many other publications from China to Brazil. Much of this coverage identified the connection between the Zuckerberg and Pelosi videos: 'A fake Zuckerberg video challenges Facebook's rules' (Metz 2019); 'Zuckerberg must tolerate the deepfake treatment' (Shand-Baptiste 2019); 'Doctored video of sinister Mark Zuckerberg puts Facebook to the test' (O'Neil 2019).

As a satire which had hit a particular target, this video focused attention and crystallized concerns about the power of social media firms, their uses of users' personal information, and the dangers of viral content, as well as demonstrating the state-of-the-art in synthetic media production. It worked on more than one level: the content of the video itself, with its *what-did-he-just-say* Zuckerberg speech, was explicitly about data and power. While the context is satirical, Zuckerberg does indeed control billions of people's data, as he is made to say in the video. The artists add the crucial word *stolen* to this observation, again highlighting questions of consent. Do social media users give meaningful informed consent for the ways their data are used when they click *OK* on the download screen? And should those users in fact be in this position? To put social media users in a situation where they have to consent to such unknowable operations, with such unknowable long-term consequences, sets them up to be victim-blamed. As Bill Posters puts it:

> The fact that citizens' data – including intimate knowledge on political leanings, sexuality, psychological traits and personality – are made available to the highest bidder shows that the digital influence industry and its associated architectures pose a risk not only to individual human rights but to our democracies at large. (Posters & Howe 2019c)

At the same time, the video's form, as a synthetic appropriation of an identifiable individual, showed Zuckerberg to be as vulnerable to having his image manipulated as anyone else. If it can happen to him, it can happen to anyone. It can happen to you. And the clip's viral circulation across the digital media environment set these same questions of data and power in the very context where they most matter. Facebook, perhaps to its credit, or perhaps in recognition that removing it would provoke a new wave of criticism and snark, elected to leave the video available rather than remove it. Six months later, the company released a formal policy on manipulated and synthetic media which allowed exemptions for satirical content (see Bickert 2020; Ajder & Glick 2021).

For the 'Big Dada/Public Faces' project, Posters and Howe worked with Israeli start-up Canny AI, a commercial firm that offers 'video dialogue replacement' (VDR) services. Using the deep learning techniques outlined in Chapter 1, Canny AI can merge sourced dialogue with an original video of the target: in this case, a speech given by Zuckerberg in 2017 about abuses of Facebook in election campaigns (Cole 2019c). Canny AI's networks were trained on source images of a voice actor performing the artists' script, and on a clip of the original target Zuckerberg talk. The result is visually convincing. But ironically, the weakest element is one of the most human ones: Zuckerberg's voice. The voice actor's performance of Zuckerberg is much less persuasive than the visual AI recreation of his facial movements and delivery. We'll explore questions of synthetic audio in more detail in Chapter 4.

Canny AI's VDR technique is an important component of the contemporary deepfake spectrum, and the basic principle of which it is an example should continue to be a significant approach. That principle is remixing a single subject. Rather than remixing the faces of two subjects, by swapping the faces of an actor with a porn star or a singer with a politician, VDR allows for a synthetic remix of a single person's image. It allows the creator to capture the authentic mannerisms, lip movements, and expressions of their target for use in delivering a new text. Rather than merging one subject with another, the VDR approach merges Zuckerberg with Zuckerberg. It remixes his own actual facial movements to match video of his mouth with a new script of words that he has not actually spoken. A video containing the new scripted dialogue becomes the source, and an existing video becomes the target. So in this example, an authentic video of Zuckerberg is processed using deep learning techniques so that his mouth now moves appropriately for the new added dialogue.

Canny AI promotes this technique as a way of localizing the dialogue of TV shows, advertisements, or corporate presentations by replacing the original voice with one in the local language, while keeping the original actor or presenter. In this sense, VDR is a sophisticated dubbing tool. But its use by artists such as Posters and Howe points to more creative, legitimate, and educational uses of synthetic media than those we discussed in Chapter 2 – uses that go beyond dubbing. 'There's a lot of hype [...] around the fake news with this technology,' Canny AI co-founder Omer Ben-Ami told one interviewer, 'and we wanted to do something with a strong unifying message, to show some positive uses for this technology' (quoted in Seymour 2019).

To demonstrate this benign potential of the technology, Canny AI introduced VDR by releasing a video in April 2019 of an ensemble of world leaders singing John Lennon's 'Imagine'. 'What you are about to see is not real,' it begins. 'But it can be.' The video then presents itself as a global media event, with images of the then-leaders of China, Iran, Japan, Russia, North Korea, Canada, Israel, the UK, and both Trump and Obama from the US, each taking a line of the song in performing a moment of global harmony. Each leader's moment in the video is performed on a different kind of screen for a different audience. Shots of each politician singing their line direct to camera are intercut with shots of audiences marvelling at this moment on TVs and phones, at home and in bars, or gathered in streets before vast urban screens. Xi Jinping trades lines with Barack Obama, while Benjamin Netanyahu and Hassan Rouhani appear side-by-side on adjacent screens in the street, singing together as a couple stop below to look up. The video presents itself as a media moment about media moments, as a video about how we watch videos.

The moment it depicts is spectacular and fantastic, but the video sets this moment in deliberately banal contexts of daily viewing. In this way, it is a careful attempt to make deepfake video seem a normal part of our everyday media lives.

The production of the 'Imagine' video involved training existing footage of each leader to sync with John Lennon's vocal delivery, before selecting the best results for each politician (Seymour 2019). The results are most effective and striking with those leaders who are not commonly seen speaking – or singing – in English, such as Xi Jinping and Kim Jong-un. This video is a powerful example of a distinct current within synthetic media of using the technology to make people aware of its possibilities: to both promote and warn. It aligns with the various examples in this book of political deepfakes made to caution the viewer about the risks of political deepfakes. The 'Imagine' video at the same time calls attention to itself as artificial ('What you are about to see is not real') and celebrates its own potential to convince ('But it can be').

This tension is one that Jay David Bolter and Richard Grusin identified in their book *Remediation* (1999). They argue that digital media are used to increase our experience of *immediacy*: the sense that we are actually there and taking part, and that this experience is above all unmediated. But at the same time, digital media also display what Bolter and Grusin call *hypermediacy*, as the media form calls attention to itself as being mediated. So using Bolter and Grusin's analysis, the 'Imagine' video calls attention to itself as a staged and hyper-mediated moment ('What you are about to see is not real'). Everything we see on our screens is taking place, within the world of that video, on other screens, as the deepfaked leaders appear on ordinary people's phones, tablets, and TVs, and as we watch those audiences viewing and participating in this imagined moment of global harmony. The obvious novelty of the images proposes them as an enhanced form of representation, as an improved model of communication that we are supposed to notice and admire. The video showcases and celebrates its own technical accomplishment. Yet at the same time, the 'Imagine' video works hard to make itself seem immediate and authentic. It connects our digital landscape of ubiquitous screens with its own, by presenting shots of audiences engaging with its deepfaked images on their own devices, inviting a more intimate and a more present recognition from us. The juxtaposition of the simulated leaders and their simulated audiences is designed to suggest that we get past the simulations and join in. The video invites us to accept our implied position as just one more of the many audiences we see in the clip, and that we recognize 'Imagine' as an authentic media moment ('But it can be').

The final Bill Posters synthetic media artwork I want to discuss in this chapter is his 'Foundation Series' (Posters 2021b). These are five character studies of what he calls 'the founding fathers of surveillance capitalism', the originators of today's trillion-dollar digital platforms: Jeff Bezos, Sergei Brin, Bill Gates, Steve Jobs, and Mark Zuckerberg. For each piece, Posters selected an early picture of that person and ran it through a neural network for tens of thousands of iterations until a hyper-realistic representation of the subject emerged. The 'Foundation Series' is different from Posters' other deepfake projects in that the focus is on the *process* of synthetic media creation rather than the end result. Where the 'Big Data/Public Faces' project was built around the final convincing simulation of the recognizable individual, the 'Foundation Series' instead highlights the creative process of image recognition and representation, and proposes this as a metaphor for our own digital condition.

In his talk at the Aesthetica Art Prize symposium in 2021, Posters (2021a) described how the Bill Gates image emerged through 80,000 iterations, using an untrained network that drew on ever-finer levels of data in learning how to see, recognize, and represent Gates's face in super-high resolution. Presented as both a video and a photographic contact sheet of thirty images from throughout the process, the artwork uses computer vision technologies to reveal the development of algorithmic power in the digital media environment. The gradual emergence of the image of Bezos or Zuckerberg, as the network learns to recognize and reproduce them, captures how each of us in turn also becomes a data image over time, as the digital platforms controlled by these figures generate an ever more detailed representation of who we are, what we do, and what we want, through our constant generation of ever more data for their analysis.

Bringing back the dead

Marcel Duchamp is not the only dead artist to be reanimated through synthetic media. The Salvador Dalí Museum in St Petersburg, Florida, created a synthetic Dalí installation called 'Dalí Lives' in 2019, thirty years after the artist's death. The result is presented on large screens throughout the museum, on which a life-size deepfake Dalí greets and interacts with visitors. At the end of each exchange, he invites the viewer to pose for a selfie with him, turning around on screen to snap a group portrait with his visitors, who can receive their selfie-with-Dalí by text message.

The museum commissioned a San Francisco advertising agency to develop this synthetic Dalí experience for its visitors. In his lifetime, Dalí appeared on television and film many times, so there is a substantial archive of footage. From the available Dalí film and video material, the project team extracted a training set of 6,000 images of the artist which went through more than 1,000 hours of neural network processing:

> In order to actually train this AI to reproduce Dalí's likeness, we started with finding the right footage of Dalí, and then we split that up into frames where he's looking the right way, and we picked the best frames to use for training from that. Our system learns exactly what he looks like, and how his mouth moves, and how his eyes move, and his eyebrows, and every little detail about what makes Dalí Dalí. (Dalí Museum 2019a)

The creators also drew upon the published archive of Dalí's own words and used a voice actor to perform a large selection of these. The synthetic images and audio recordings were combined into 125 short videos totalling forty-five minutes. The synthetic Dalí is able to respond to comments and questions, with a claimed 190,512 possible combinations of the videos available to fashion each individual interaction (Dalí Museum 2019a).

The deepfake Dalí is quite a charming creation. The playful interactions programmed for visitors make possible new moments of connection with Dalí's art, and perhaps provoke reflections on mortality too. The synthetic Dalí has the effect of humanizing him. And Dalí, it seems probable, might have liked this use of his words and image. He might have appreciated the provocation, the humour, the avant-garde creativity, and the way it contributes to the professional brand that he was tireless in cultivating while alive. Dalí's art itself also made important use of appropriation of found objects as a strategy. Among his best-known works, for instance, is the 1938 assemblage 'Lobster Telephone', combining a fake lobster with a real telephone. Given that this synthetic creation was made by the Dalí Museum, the official Dalí industry, one has to imagine that the Dalí estate are on board with this. But as with the deepfake porn videos discussed in Chapter 2, the apparently more benign Dalí case also shows how the uses of synthetic media technologies centre on questions of consent. Salvador Dalí has not consented to these uses of his face, words, or celebrity image any more than Emma Watson has to the abuse of hers (see also Mihailova 2021).

The 'Dalí Lives' project plays with concepts of immortality and death. The entire concept is like a weird séance. Bringing back the dead is a mainstay of the demonstration of new visual technologies, and best articulates the convergence of the digital and the magical, of the celebration of a specific technology and the suspension of disbelief. One of the project's promotional videos opens with Dalí's final public statement: 'When you are a genius, you do not have the right to die, because we are necessary for the progress of humanity' (Dalí Museum 2019a). Another ends with the reanimated artist looking straight at the viewer to flatly deny his own death:

> I have a long-standing relationship with death – almost thirty years. I, in life, always believed the desire to survive and the fear of death were artistic sentiments. I

understand that better now. But there is one thing that makes me different. I do not believe in my death. Do you? (Dalí Museum 2019b)

But there is also something unsettling and eerie about reanimating the dead. And there is something undignified about licensing a zombie Salvador Dalí to market and promote a museum and its accompanying participation in the commercial art and tourism industries. Does his status as an artist, or his celebrity, or the thirty-year gap since his death make reanimating Dalí different from reanimating someone you used to go out with? Where might we draw the line?

The first stirrings of reanimating people from our own pasts can be seen in the 'Deep Nostalgia' tool offered by genealogy company MyHeritage. It uses deep learning techniques to animate old family photos. Upload a picture of a long-dead relative whom you never met and Deep Nostalgia will make them smile, tilt their head, look at the person next to them in the photo, blow you a kiss, or apply various other animations that the software processes as a good match for your chosen subject. The effect is rather like an image from a newspaper in a *Harry Potter* movie or a more emphatic version of the 'live' photos that can be captured on iPhones. Like the deepfake Dalí, it simultaneously reaches back to imagined pasts and to prehistories of media spectacle, while also pointing to more elaborate possibilities as such techniques develop. Questions of consent in relation to synthetic media may become everyday questions that we will all encounter in future.

The makers of the ancillary *Star Wars* film *Rogue One* (2016) cast the late British actor Peter Cushing to reprise his role from the first *Star Wars* film of 1977. Cushing's role in *Rogue One* came more than twenty years after his death in 1994, and at a time when he would have been over a hundred years old had he lived. The effects firm Industrial Light & Magic filmed a different actor performing the part, then digitally sutured Cushing's face into the footage (Cavna 2016). This deliberate casting of a long-dead performer is quite different from analogous cases where a film had to be salvaged through digital effects when a key actor died during production, as happened with Paul Walker in *Furious 7* (2015), Oliver Reed in *Gladiator* (2000), and Brandon Lee in *The Crow* (1994). The *Star Wars* franchise also crafted a posthumous performance from the late Carrie Fisher, repurposing unused footage for *The Rise of Skywalker* (2019).

In the final film before her death, Fisher was also digitally de-aged for the climax of *Rogue One*. De-ageing technology has become a key application of synthetic effects, with virtual make-up effects used on Michael Douglas in *Ant-Man* and *Avengers* films, and on Robert DeNiro and Al Pacino in Martin Scorsese's *The Irishman* (2019) (Desowitz 2019; Golding 2021). The use of de-ageing technology to insert the young Mark Hamill as Luke Skywalker into the climax of Disney's TV series *The Mandalorian* prompted one deepfake creator to make their own version and exhibit the two side-by-side on their YouTube channel. This amateur deepfake was so clearly superior to the effects achieved by Lucasfilm that they hired its creator (Baxter 2021; see also Holliday 2021).

Digital reanimations are authorized by those with whom the late performer was most closely connected while alive. Singer Natalie Cole won two Grammys for 'Unforgettable' in 1991, on which she duetted with her father, Nat King Cole, who had by then been dead for more than twenty-five years. To promote their 1995

97

career retrospective TV and album series *Anthology*, the surviving Beatles recorded their first new material in a quarter of a century by developing fragments of two home demos recorded by John Lennon a few years before his death. The first track released, 'Free As a Bird', became a new Beatles song with lead vocals by a member who had been dead for fifteen years and had not consented to again collaborate with the band that had disintegrated in acrimony a decade before his death. While Lennon's estate endorsed this, and indeed facilitated it by sharing the demos, there is once more something undignified about the results. Again, questions of consent are central to the use of someone's voice, image, or face.

Such questions arise beyond the sphere of popular entertainment. Issues of consent have also been raised around the use of synthetic media to reanimate a murdered journalist in Mexico as part of an activist intervention. Activist group Propuesta Civica used deepfakes to resurrect Javier Valdez Cárdenas three years after his death. His likeness was used in a campaign that they believed he would have supported in life (Ajder & Glick 2021: 19). AI activist Mutale Nkonde has strongly criticized this as a colonialist act that wrongly equates an individual's work with their personhood (WITNESS 2021).

Synthetic media are part of a wider canvas of efforts to maintain the presence of the dead, whether for spiritual, emotional, or nakedly commercial reasons. So-called holographic effects (more accurately 3D projections) have also been used to reanimate the dead. For his wife Kim Kardashian's fortieth birthday, Kanye West commissioned a message from her late father using such technology. Her reanimated dad reassured her that she had married 'the most, most, most, most,

most genius man in the whole world' (Gorman 2020). Rapper Tupac Shakur, murdered in 1996, performed onstage at the Coachella music festival sixteen years later in a similar optical illusion. Controversial plans for a concert tour featuring a projected version of the late Amy Winehouse backed by a live band almost a decade after her death were put on hold in 2019 amidst ethical concerns about the singer's inability to consent and about whether potential motion-capture models had been made fully aware of that role when auditioning for the tour (Snapes 2019).

Such appearances are contemporary descendants of nineteenth-century optical illusions such as the *done-with-mirrors* Pepper's Ghost, which was first exhibited in 1862 as part of the regular public science activities and theatrical spectacles that animated the Royal Polytechnic Institution in London (much later to become the University of Westminster) (Brooker 2009). Scientific and technological advances are often expressed as spectacular imagery, often in science fiction genres. In those contexts, they frequently connect to futurist visions of technological dystopias that help to shape popular conceptions of the future itself. Michele Pierson (2002) argues that the public presentation of such novel imagery as Pepper's Ghost and other nineteenth-century spectacles, combined with their discussion in popular science magazines and other media, helped develop the public appetite for special effects that has now driven Hollywood cinema for thirty years. The label Pepper's *Ghost* also makes explicit the connections between visual technology, spiritualism, and ideas of communicating with the dead.

So one way of viewing synthetic media is as a genre of special effects. The special effects film is of course most often science fiction, the genre that has always most closely expressed cultural attitudes towards technology. Andrew Murphie and John Potts (2003) point out that science fiction is significant for its explorations and expressions of contemporary cultural values about technology, rather than for its projections of the future. Michele Pierson (2002) identifies histories of contemporary cinematic special effects, tracing their antecedents in stagecraft and theatrical magic, in modelling and stop-motion animation, in pyrotechnics, make-up, and prosthetics. She points to connections between CGI and the light and stage magic shows of the early nineteenth century. Carolyn Marvin (1988) has described the excitement around electric light at that time, and how its uses in public spectacle seemed to prefigure a whole new era of electric light communication. Pierson also traces contemporary special effects to popular science exhibits and displays, and popular science publications from *Scientific American* to *Wired* magazine, as engines of the ongoing public fascination with the convergence of science and spectacle.

Parallel to reanimating the dead, synthetic media and related visual effects technologies are also being used to experiment with the creation of new virtual characters and performers. China's state-run Xinhua news agency has experimented with developing virtual news presenters, demonstrating prototype AI news anchors in 2018 (Baraniuk 2018). By 2021, such experiments had already become considerably more convincing, with South Korea's MBN news channel showing off a virtual version of news anchor Kim Joo-Ha that prompted some viewers to express concerns that she might lose her job (Debusmann 2021). Virtual singers and pop performers have a longer history, playing on fans' expectations in a similar way to precedents reaching back to the 1960s such as cartoon band Josie and the Pussycats or cosplay act the Banana Splits. Pop celebrity is often best understood as a manufactured product, with a key twenty-first-century innovation being the development of reality TV contests that enlisted the audience as a massive focus group, collaborating in designing the product that would be sold to them at the end of the season. Computer-generated idols take this manufacture of celebrity literally, and have attracted massive investment and experimentation since the 1990s (St Michel 2016). Japanese virtual idol Hatsune Miku has done sold-out international arena tours as a stage projection, opening for Lady Gaga and performing with a live band at Coachella.

Virtual YouTubers (VTubers) and Instagram influencers also use digital technology to animate characters such as Prada's Candy for branding and marketing, with new models being launched frequently (track their fortunes at www.virtualhumans.org). VTubers and Twitch streamers from Kizuna AI to CodeMiko are developed by talent agencies and can draw billions of views. Established virtual Instagram influencer Lil Miquela had over 3 million followers as of October 2021 for posts that mix sponsored content for luxury brands into a low-concept mystery narrative about how the character discovered it was 'a robot' after being hacked. One industry estimate has brands spending up to US$15billion a year on influencer marketing by 2022, with virtual influencers accounting for an increasing share of this (Ong 2020). Virtual influencer Imma, for example, has appeared in expensive promotional campaigns such as one in which the character's narrative has it settling in to a new home that turns out to be inside the Harajuku Ikea store. These virtual influencers exploit the potential of networked digital media and their convergence of branded public content with personal communication across platforms from Twitch to Chaturbate. The presence of Chaturbate in that last sentence reminds us from Chapter 2 of the gendered nature of so much synthetic media, with a sexualized VTuber called Projekt Melody building a lucrative profile on its Pornhub channel (Faber 2021).

Brilliant disguise

Welcome to Chechnya is a 2020 documentary film directed by David France that makes ground-breaking use of deepfake approaches in order to achieve a unique kind of realism. The film explores victims and activists responding to the organized persecution at the state level of LGBTQ people in Chechnya. From its premiere at Sundance in 2020, it has been featured at numerous film festivals worldwide and given a release through HBO. *Welcome to Chechnya* follows survivors of violent persecution for their sexuality and the efforts of a network of supporters to get them out of the country to safety. We observe these victims living in safe houses while preparing to flee the country, and we watch unbearably tense sequences in airports, filmed covertly on smartphones, as some attempt their escapes. Given the life-threatening context, the director had extraordinary levels of access to these people, but faced ethical quandaries in deciding how to represent them on screen without further endangering them. Standard documentary techniques such as blurring faces or filming them in shadows work to reduce the humanity of the person on screen rather than convey it to the viewer in the way that France wanted. The solution was synthetic media. 'For their safety,' reads a caption in the opening scene, 'people fleeing for their lives have been digitally disguised.'

In a filmed interview (WITNESS 2020b), France described how he explored a number of options, including Rotoscoping, a technique that traces over filmed images to render them as a kind of animation. But the results didn't provide enough of a disguise for the subjects and weren't equal to the gravity of the situation in the film. In looking for an alternative solution, his team discovered the Nicolas Cage faceset that has been used to create so many deepfake movie parodies. They tested it on video of one of the film's key protagonists and were excited that he was rendered entirely anonymous behind Cage's face, while at the same time preserving his own expressions and movements. So France and his collaborators then worked with Hollywood visual effects specialist Ryan Laney to develop a machine-learning system they called a 'face veil'. The filmmakers recruited more than twenty volunteer LGBTQ activists in the US whose faces are mapped over those of the actual victims who feature in the documentary; in some cases volunteers also provided voiceovers to disguise the voices of the people in the film. This is not best understood as a performance – instead, as Laney has put it, these volunteer activists are 'effectively acting as a human shield' (quoted in Hao 2020a). The technical achievement is deeply impressive: France notes that eighty minutes of the film feature face-veiled subjects, and that they are not static talking heads, but are moving around and interacting with others while preserving the synthetic effect. These subjects are given a subtle glow effect on screen to remind the viewer at all times that they are disguised for their safety.

For this documentary, synthetic media provided a kind of mask or prosthetic disguise that enables the film to maintain the authenticity and realism of its hand-held footage shot in often tense and dangerous situations, while still protecting the identities of its subjects. David France hails the face-veil technique as a major advance in documentary filmmaking, saying, 'It gives people back their voice through someone else's skin' (quoted in Thomson 2020). The technology is also used as a dramatic device when one of the subjects of the film chooses to step out from behind their digital mask to appear as their real self at a media conference that becomes a pivotal moment in the documentary – this moment of unveiling is both a crucial development in the film's narrative and a revelation to the viewer about what they have been watching. France rejects the term *deepfake* for his work on *Welcome to Chechnya*. 'Deepfake is the crime, not the technology,' he told one interviewer (WITNESS 2020b), suggesting that its use in the film would be better described as *deeptruth*.

Trumping the president

The US presidency of Donald Trump was in many ways far beyond satire. His entire term in office itself appeared to be satirical: a deliberate inversion of norms and expectations of the presidency. Trump performed as a lord of misrule. His term placed itself so far beyond any established take on how a presidency should be conducted that it's hard for any satirist to go further. Where could a satirist start with Trump's suggestion that Covid-19 patients should be injected with bleach? What image could be weirder and more deflating of the presidency than that of Trump grinning demonically in a candle-lit White House dining room, surrounded by towers of hundreds of McDonald's burgers for his guests? What could be more grotesque than him physically mocking a disabled journalist on camera? What parody could puncture his use of the presidency more than his appeal on television to Russia for help in hacking Hillary Clinton's emails? How could a satirist get started on Trump's custom of closing his rallies by dad-dancing to 'Y.M.C.A.'? Whether he was enlisting to his cause Vladimir Putin, or the insurrectionist mob at the Capitol on 6 January 2021, or the entire electoral apparatus of the Republican Party, Trump always found ways to subvert and undermine the office of the presidency that satire couldn't match.

So rather than trying to outdo Trump's words in excess, the tactic of the most effective satirists of his era was to use his own exact words themselves. US comedian Sarah Cooper built a substantial following for a series of TikTok videos in which she lip-synced to Trump's latest outrage. UK actor and comic voice artist Peter Serafinowicz took a similar approach in his YouTube series of 'Sassy Trump' videos, where the key was again that the words were all authentic Trump moments – not scripted satire, but a taunting echo of the president's own words respoken with a camp accent and delivery that punctured Trump's leering, gravelly cadences. Again the distinction between remixing texts and remixing contexts is useful: these videos were a remix of the context in which Trump's words appear, not of the text of those words.

Serafinowicz's 'Sassy Trump' accent was to become the basis of 'Sassy Justice', a fifteen-minute deepfake YouTube video created with Trey Parker and Matt Stone, the team behind *South Park* and *Team America: World Police*. 'Sassy Justice' uses state-of-the-art synthetic media to digitally superimpose Trump's face on a different character, that of local TV journalist Fred Sassy,

played by Serafinowicz. The character of Sassy syntheti-
cally remixes Donald Trump's face on to Serafinowicz's
performance, adding a curly white hairstyle. The video
combines sophisticated deepfake techniques with crude
puppets and parodies of low-budget local TV ads, using
the same distinctive mix of laser-like satire and childish
playground humour that has been familiar to *South
Park* viewers for more than twenty years.

'Sassy Justice' is itself themed around deepfakes:
'Scammers are finding new ways to take advantage
of you, the consumer. Now, with a technology called
deepfake, you can get screwed over and lied to in ways
never before possible.' Throughout, Sassy interviews
various fictional experts about the risks of synthetic
media and tries out a detection tool, built into an
actual tinfoil hat. The show's creators saw it as a
project where they could learn how to make deepfakes
while simultaneously demystifying them for the viewer
(Itzkoff 2020). 'Sassy Justice' was salvaged from a
feature-length deepfake film project that was derailed
by the arrival of the Covid-19 pandemic. For that
abandoned project, Parker and Stone had launched a
synthetic film studio called Deep Voodoo, hiring some
twenty deepfake creators, and making 'Sassy Justice',
in Parker's words, 'probably the single most expensive
YouTube video ever made' (quoted in Itzkoff 2020).
It was followed by a five-minute Christmas episode of
Trump reading a children's story.

'Sassy Justice' is proof-of-concept for deepfakes as
entertainment. The technology works in the episode
both as a form of animation and as a form of costuming
or make-up. Its high-profile creators and the investment
in Deep Voodoo have the effect of professionalizing
what had previously been a niche area of amateurs
uploading Nicolas Cage synthetic mash-ups to YouTube.

Much of that earlier work turned out to be showreels for their creators, just as 'Sassy Justice' itself turns out to be something of a showreel for Parker, Stone, and Serafinowicz, who joked to the *New York Times* that they were hoping for a call from Steven Spielberg. Prominent YouTube deepfakers Ctrl Shift Face and derpfakes both announced on their Twitter profiles that they had been recruited to Deep Voodoo. Both had built catalogues of synthetic movie and music video remixes, recasting Willem Dafoe as Hannibal Lecter, David Bowie as Rick Astley, or Nicolas Cage as almost everyone. Also recruited to Deep Voodoo was Chris Ume, whose @deeptomcruise TikTok account showcased some very high-quality deepfakes of Cruise in 2021 (Venkataramakrishnan 2021).

'Sassy Justice' cuts-and-pastes Trump's image into a fictional local news broadcast, reimagining him as the self-important host of a consumer advocacy current affairs show in Cheyenne, Wyoming. As well as Fred Sassy, 'Sassy Justice' features synthetic versions of Trump himself, his daughter Ivanka, and her husband, Jared Kushner, deepfaked here as a small, Holocaust-denying child. The deepfaked Trump is shown having a stroke while being interviewed by Chris Wallace of Fox News: 'Mr Trump, are you having a stroke right now? Or are you just making fun of people with disabilities?' There are also segments with deepfakes of actors Julie Andrews and Michael Caine (unlikely choices, perhaps driven by the ability of Serafinowicz and his partner to do good voice impressions of both), former US Vice-President Al Gore, and Mark Zuckerberg. At the same time, the video mocks cultural anxieties by presenting what the viewer is told will be convincing deepfakes of actor Tom Cruise or singer Carrie Underwood, but which turn out to be cheap-looking cloth puppets. Call it fake news.

There was an earlier sense of 'fake news' long before Trump weaponized the term as a device to dismiss or delegitimize any information or source that did not contribute to his agenda. There was considerable popular and academic attention in the Bush and Obama years towards the kinds of parodic fake TV news produced by Jon Stewart or Stephen Colbert in the US, by Chris Morris and Armando Iannucci in the UK, by *The Chaser* team in Australia, and by comparable creators and commentators around the world, as well as towards the print and online output of *The Onion* and its many imitators (Baym & Jones 2013). Satire, by which I mean art on the attack, has long played a crucial role in highlighting and challenging the conventions of the news, and how these are used to construct a position of authority over its audiences: the stylized gravitas of the newsreader; the portentous theme music; the endless sense of urgency; the defining perspectives of the highest-status voices; and the use of graphics and visuals to structure each story (and to exclude any story that lacks the right visuals).

It's significant that 'Sassy Justice' is satirical, that it uses the possibilities offered by the emerging technology to undermine that very technology, that this kind of criticism of synthetic media emerges at the same time as those media. Its combination of sophisticated synthetic media, cheap TV graphics, and rubbish puppets showcases the deepfake techniques more effectively than a straight deepfake might. It draws attention to how it achieves its effects even as it works to convince you that it's real. Here again there are modernist precursors in remix aesthetics. For a prehistory of 'Sassy Justice', consider the satirical photomontages of the Berlin Dada period. Those artists – John Heartfield, Raoul Hausmann, Hannah Höch – 'use distortion to expose truth' (Gale 1997: 131). Photomontage drew on what was then the new availability of photos. The Dadaists' work took shape as newspapers, magazines, and advertisements proliferated with the emergence of what we used to call mass media. For the first time, photos were everywhere and cheap to obtain. Berlin Dadaists, observes Kuenzli, were early to the idea of artistic interventions against the media: 'Replacing their paintbrushes and paint with scissors and glue, they cut up newspapers and illustrated magazines, recontexual-izing these fragments: reality as fixed by society is either dissolved or exposed in these works' (2006: 92). In their hands, the photomontage strategy became 'a joke at the expense of realism' (Bigsby 1972: 19).

The Dada use of photos was immediate when compared to the fragments of menus or train tickets in earlier collages, but was also hypermediated by the emphasis on juxtaposition. Hannah Höch's 1919 photomontage 'Cut with the Kitchen Knife through the Last Epoch of Weimar Beer-Belly Culture in Germany' is a dense, fantastic collage of imagery: animals, machines, and crowds juxtaposed with images of artists, of Lenin and Einstein, and of the repeated newsprint word *Dada*. The surface realism of the photos offers both immediate familiarity (*there's Marx*) and disorientation (*is that a tapir?*). It's a challenge and an invitation, a gesture that acknowledges the new image environment of the twentieth century, and its possibilities and threats.

Hausmann's 'The Art Critic' (1919–20) is a photomontage that combines the immediate realism of photography with the hypermediation of the collage aesthetic. A male figure fills the centre of the image against an orange poster. Childlike drawings of blazing eyes and a scowling mouth are superimposed on the figure's broken-veined face. He holds a sharpened pencil as though ready for a knife-fight, looking past a woman's head on the right of the image, and a man's silhouette cut out of newsprint. There are fragments of banknotes and advertising images of shoes, stabbing him in the back of the neck and stamped on his forehead. In Bolter and Grusin's terms, the use of photographs for the heads of the central figure and the woman is immediate, but the overall effect of the montage is hypermediated: it calls attention to itself as an image, and demands to be read as a dense combination of remixed found material.

These kinds of photomontage became possible because there were more photos than ever, and because those photos were cheap and accessible as raw material. In a parallel way, deepfakes are possible because there are now more digital photos and videos than ever, and these too are now cheap and accessible as raw material. The parallel between the Dada moment and our own is the sudden acceleration in content, the mass availability of visual images and digital data. A century of cut-and-paste cultures has made appropriation, remixing, and sharing into normal and everyday activities. And the biggest digital firms continue to drive this, from the annual introduction of new smartphone cameras to the constant addition of new image filters and apps. A century later, 'Sassy Justice' is very much in this Dada tradition of using media tools and the glut of available images to play with new possibilities for self-reflexive media satire.

As satire, 'Sassy Justice' provides a significant perspective on the 2020 US presidential election, the roles of deepfakes in that election, and the wider problems of trust and the media. Many had expected that election to spawn serious deepfakes, but the real issues of trust and credibility instead came more simply from Trump repeatedly saying on Twitter and on TV that the election had been stolen from him. The 'Sassy Justice' five-minute December episode parodies this by having Serafinowicz's deepfake Trump read a children's story about a reindeer who loses an election to a corrupt opponent, despite everyone in the forest agreeing he was 'the best reindeer ever'. So this actual election deepfake is a parody of the real election trust crisis, with the twist that the actual election trust crisis didn't actually need synthetic media to convince Trump's followers.

Life hacking

Several 'Sassy Justice' segments feature mock TV commercials with Mark Zuckerberg as local business figure 'The Dialysis King', offering two-for-one deals on kidney treatment, and promising financing options against people's mortgages or other assets:

> Are you feeling run down? Have you been diagnosed with Type 1 or Type 2 kidney failure? Then come on down to Cheyenne Dialysis! We got all the deals, and all the customers, that made me the Dialysis King of Cheyenne. Both kidney dialysis just $89,999! Two-day full kidney dialysis, $199,999! At these prices, you can't afford *not* to get dialysis! No insurance? No problem! We'll work with you, using your mortgage, will or other assets. Stop being a burden on your family, and come get dialysis today! And don't get it from anyone but the Dialysis King.

These segments are expert parodies of the conventions of low-budget TV commercials – the stock music, the cheap graphics, the rushed voiceover disclaimers – and this hypermediated satire contrasts very effectively with the sophistication of the deepfake representation of Zuckerberg. On one level, this is just daft and childish, with the synthetic Zuckerberg appearing in a turkey costume and a bra in different segments. But at the same time it does actually point towards something important in relation to social media and the digital environment: the idea that the big digital firms are all moving into healthcare in different ways because there are new streams of data there to be exploited, and anything that has not been mediated before now is of interest. The decision to make fun of Mark Zuckerberg as though he were a predatory health service provider captures something about contemporary digital media that is not always fully recognized.

All of the most prominent digital corporations have begun to establish themselves in the health sector: Alphabet/Google, Apple, Meta/Facebook, Amazon, and Microsoft. Health services offer these firms new sources of data and so new streams of revenue. Amazon, Microsoft, and Google offer cloud services and provide AI analytics to health services (Ofcom 2021: 127). Health tracking and monitoring sensors and apps are increasingly integrated into everyday devices such as smartphones and wearable technologies such as watches or fitness wristbands (Bunz & Meikle 2018). The giant digital platforms can no longer get by on harvesting just our pictures, videos, contacts, and opinions. Their relentless logic of data extraction means that they now need to monitor, track, and analyse our body-fat levels, emotional states, daily step-counts, menstrual cycles, heart rates, alcohol intake, and sleeping patterns.

To take just a few examples, Facebook launched a preventive health tool in the US in 2020 which encourages users to track and record health data so that the platform can connect them with commercial partners, including 'affordable places to access health care near you' (https://preventivehealth.facebook. com). Google bought fitness tracker company Fitbit in late 2019 for US$2.1 billion, not just integrating that company's devices and software to Google's systems, but also buying control over Fitbit's user data and extensive network of third-party data-tracking and analysis apps (BBC News 2020b). Amazon owns and operates pharmacy service PillPack in the US, giving it nationwide licences to deliver prescription medicines and integrated connections with pharmaceutical corporations and health insurance companies. There is no area of our lives that these companies will not mine in order to extract our most personal, most intimate data. The sheer inescapability of this oligopoly means that this is a machine, as Foucault said of surveillance, 'in which everyone is caught' (1980: 156). Deepfakes are an outcome of this environment, and of these business models, in which all lived experience becomes data for analysis and exploitation.

Summary

This chapter has focused on some of the positive creative potential of deepfake media, exploring case studies whose intentions and uses should perhaps not be described as deep*fakes* at all (which is one reason I use the term *synthetic media* so much in this book, even if most of the creators discussed in this chapter do use *deepfake* to describe their work). As happens with every new technical medium, artists have quickly gravitated towards synthetic media to experiment with their potential. Many of those experiments can be seen in a longer historical timeline as part of the remix creativity that became central to so much art and creative production in the twentieth century, from Dada to hip hop, from cinema editing to jazz. As with the deepfake porn videos of Chapter 2, the examples in this chapter highlight the importance of questions of consent as synthetic media use develops. Some of the more prominent and high-profile synthetic media projects are also very self-reflexive, using deepfakes to publicize, interrogate, or critique the possibilities of deepfakes, and to question the social media contexts and practices that make those deepfake approaches possible.

4

Manipulating Trust

Everyone who was alive in 1969 can remember the exact moment when they learned of the deaths on the moon of astronauts Neil Armstrong and Buzz Aldrin. Those of us too young to remember have still seen the news film countless times, and have known our whole lives that the Apollo 11 mission that should have seen people walk on the moon for the first time instead ended in tragedy. The televised address that night by US President Richard Nixon still resonates more than half a century on:

> Fate has ordained that the men who went to the moon to explore in peace will stay on the moon to rest in peace. These brave men, Neil Armstrong and Edwin Aldrin, know that there is no hope for their recovery. But they also know that there is hope for mankind in their sacrifice. These two men are laying down their lives in mankind's most noble goal: the search for truth and understanding.

Not how you remember it? Of course, Armstrong and Aldrin returned safely from walking on the moon in 1969, along with third Apollo 11 crew member Michael Collins, and both lived long into the twenty-first century. But the speech was real – it was just never delivered. Nixon's speechwriter William Safire wrote it for him in case it was needed. I've transcribed part of it here from the Emmy-winning deepfake video 'In Event of Moon Disaster', which reanimates Nixon to deliver that speech.

'In Event of Moon Disaster' is a deepfake art project that addresses the relationships between synthetic media, truth, and trust. It both presents and critiques the persuasive possibilities of deepfake technologies. It celebrates those possibilities in its own accomplishment, at the same time as it warns the viewer about them by showing history being rewritten on screen. It works hard to gain the viewer's trust even as it suggests that trust should be withheld. Its web version at https://moondisaster.org comes with links to extensive behind-the-scenes resources and critical discussions, making it one of the most essential deepfake examples to date.

In some ways, choosing the moon landing as the historical moment to rewrite seems not only provocative but also unwise. After all, there are already significant numbers of people who doubt it ever happened. A 1976 self-published pamphlet by one Ray Kaysing established many of the debating points still used by those who believe the moon landings were a hoax, despite their painstaking rebuttal by NASA; Kaysing's arguments were later given much wider currency when presented in a 2001 Fox News documentary (Godwin 2019). This idea of historical fakery persists. A 2019 UK survey by pollsters YouGov about belief in conspiracy theories found that 16% of respondents believed the moon landings were definitely (4%) or probably (12%)

fake – one in six of those surveyed (Waldersee 2019). Social media have provided fresh opportunities for moon-landing-deniers to connect, communicate, and collaborate. So in this context, it's not hard to imagine ways in which 'In Event of Moon Disaster' could be used to further undermine both the historical and scientific record and public trust in science and its communication.

Richard Nixon is at the same time a provocative and yet also appropriate choice for a project revolving around public trust. Nixon's career was plagued by a physical appearance of untrustworthiness that reportedly led viewers of his TV debate with John F. Kennedy to rate Kennedy the winner while those who listened on the radio rated Nixon instead (Meyrowitz 1985: 281). And of course Nixon's presidency disintegrated in flames in 1974 as he resigned on live TV while the Watergate investigations closed in on his administration, having earlier snarled on television from Disneyworld, 'I'm not a crook' (Woodward & Bernstein 1974: 334). A political leader like Nixon has access to exceptional resources of symbolic power (Thompson 1995): the capacity to name and to define, to explain, to argue, and to persuade. But even a US president is not always able to deploy those resources in a convincing way. Central to questions of symbolic power and communication is trust.

Deepfakes are emerging in a climate of a widespread erosion of trust in public institutions and public life (Davis 2019: 7–9). There are many dimensions to this, but to take just some examples in the UK context, the decaying of public trust can be observed in relation to electoral politics and government, to banking and finance, and to the media. The echoes of the 2003 invasion of Iraq, and the false prospectus that was offered to justify it,

117

augment more standard narratives around scandals and gaffes (Thompson 2000; Castells 2004). The conduct of the Vote Leave campaign in the Brexit referendum of 2016 has developed into an open disregard for truth in public discourse, as that campaign's key figures became the government that tried to suspend parliament in 2019 in order to evade its scrutiny. The global financial crisis and its aftermath have undermined trust in the banking and finance sectors, and further eroded trust in political parties and governments perceived to have protected vested interests. UK politicians themselves became seen as vested interests in the 2009 MPs' expenses scandal, which revealed widespread abuse of parliamentary expenses. (In one memorable case, an MP billed the public for having the moat around his house cleaned.) In 2021, this found a historical rhyme in the emergence of new claims of corrupt MPs paid to lobby and to award government contracts. And media industries have eroded trust in themselves, whether the established news media through high-profile scandals at the BBC or phone-hacking by Rupert Murdoch's News Corporation, or social media through the Snowden and Cambridge Analytica revelations.

Deepfakes land in all of this like a dirty bomb. Synthetic media are technologies for the creation and distribution of images, audio, and videos that challenge fundamental understandings of trust and communication. They are technologies that can be used to undermine public communication – because it's not just that we might believe something false is real, but also that we might believe something real is false. Legal scholars Bobby Chesney and Danielle Citron term this dilemma the Liar's Dividend, as they observe that 'Deep fakes will make it easier for liars to deny the truth' (2019: 1785). They also note that there is a dark paradox here, as the more the public is educated about the nature and dangers of deepfakes, the more likely it is that they can be persuaded that something real is false. (We will return to such questions of synthetic media literacy in the concluding chapter of this book.) Deepfakes are a get-out-of-jail-free card for all kinds of authoritarian communicators, who can now use the very existence of synthetic media to sow doubt over any piece of content, real or not (Gregory 2021a).

So deepfakes are a significant development in this wider erosion of trust that can be seen to be affecting media, news, and political communication. Trust is central to communication. Communication is the making of meanings – a collaborative process, even if at a distance. A writer may not know you're making meanings from what they've written, but both you and the writer are involved in the process. Trust is intimate and central to intimacy. Trust is shared, but not always: trust can be one-way or reciprocal, and can be abused or misplaced. Trust is about power, whether gaining someone's trust to influence them or giving someone your trust, and with it power over you. To trust someone is a kind of submission but also an act of agency, an expression of will. Trust is a kind of calculation in the making of meanings, whether conscious or not. We must decide, whether rationally, instinctively, or emotionally, whether to trust a message, an image, a video. In the contemporary networked digital media environment, we may not know for sure who the sender or creator of a message really is. So trust becomes a matter of confidence, belief, and faith, all of which can be abused and manipulated.

This is why it is important to understand deepfakes as part of the social media environment. Deepfakes are made possible by the practices of social media platforms and users, from the new ubiquity of digital photos that can be used to train machine-learning systems, to the algorithmic sorting and distribution of public and personal communication. Social media have brought with them all kinds of new ways in which individuals can create, remix, and manipulate media content, and they are platforms through which users can share that content. The political economy of social media platforms is also crucial to deepfakes, because their business models make those platforms reluctant to censor content and can make them promote controversial or flammable content that may be false or misleading. Deepfakes circulate through platforms that use a business model of building up a detailed profile of the user in order to target them with specific content and advertising. And because remixing digital content is easy, and because the database environment of the web makes it easy to separate content from source, users may never be certain of the source or authenticity of information that is targeted at them.

So scarcity of information and access gives way to scarcity of attention, authority, and credibility. This climate underpins much of the anxiety around so-called *fake news* (McNair 2018; Zimdars & McLeod 2020). The word *fake* is a problem in this term, as indeed it can be in the term *deepfake*. However, in this context it does help us to locate these phenomena in relation to much wider patterns of decaying public trust. This chapter examines some of the implications for public communication when our capacities to manipulate and share images and ideas outstrip our capacity to trust, and some of the key questions for trust and communication that are raised by synthetic media.

Re-recording history

'In Event of Moon Disaster' originally appeared in November 2019 as an installation at the International Documentary Film Festival Amsterdam, where it was exhibited on a TV screen within a physical space that simulated a 1969 American living room. It has since appeared at other arts festivals in several countries, and in September 2021 won the Emmy for 'Outstanding Interactive Media: Documentary'. The short film was directed by Francesca Panetta and Halsey Burgund, and produced by D. Fox Harrell of MIT. Both directors were also attached to MIT and had established track records as multimedia artists and producers. Panetta had previously led the *Guardian*'s ultimately unsuccessful efforts to develop a substantial VR news presence in 2017. The newspaper distributed 100,000 Google Cardboard VR headsets free to readers to try to drive traffic to its experimental VR story-telling such as Panetta's impressive 6×9, which put the user in simulated solitary confinement inside a US prison cell.

The deepfake elements of 'In Event of Moon Disaster' were created by Canny AI, which we encountered in Chapter 3 and which handled the deepfake visuals, and by Respeecher, a synthetic audio firm based in Ukraine that describes its work as 'Voice Cloning for Content Creators'. Respeecher worked on simulating Nixon's voice (DelViscio 2020). One thing that marks out this film as a real advance in deepfakes is that the audio and video are equally convincing. For the moon film, both firms worked with actor Lewis D. Wheeler: Canny AI to develop a convincing simulation of Nixon's facial movements as he delivers the speech; Respeecher to develop a synthetic version of the actor's voice that they could merge with their neural network trained on recordings of Nixon's voice. The filmmakers selected footage of Nixon's resignation speech in 1974 as their target because his grave tone and demeanour offered a plausible match for delivering the moon disaster speech.

The film is a sophisticated mix of real archival footage and new synthetic content, and this combination is crucial to the overall effect. Nixon's speech lasts for almost half of its six-minute duration, and its undeniable impression of authenticity is greatly enhanced by the genuine archival context material. The video begins with original footage of CBS anchor Walter Cronkite covering the Apollo 11 launch in Florida, with shots of the excited crowds and voices saying that buildings are shaking as the rocket takes off. Next we see more archival footage recorded inside the craft by the astronauts on their way to the moon. Halfway through the film, the simulation takes over: the archival footage is manipulated to suggest trouble on board the rocket; the signal appears lost and a test card is replaced by a screen announcing a CBS special report. The deepfake Nixon then delivers the synthetic version of Safire's authentic text. The level of sophistication and craft in creating 'In Event of Moon Disaster' shows just how difficult it is to make a really top-tier deepfake like this one. This film took a large and well-resourced team of creative professionals three months (Panetta & Burgund 2020). The audio alone involved a great deal of research and labour: the actor was recorded delivering hundreds of brief phrases that had been selected from recordings of authentic Nixon speeches. Respeecher's models were then trained on both versions until they could reproduce the actor's delivery of the moon disaster speech with the convincing accent, timbre, and cadences of the late president. Respeecher describe this process as 'Photoshop for voice' (Dickson 2020).

This book has mostly focused on video deepfakes, but of course audio deepfakes are important too – and their combination is one reason why 'In Event of Moon Disaster' is such an impressive example. Many of the most widely seen examples of deepfakes to date involve voice actors performing straight impersonations of their subject: Jordan Peele provided the voice for one of the earliest deepfakes to garner media attention, in which Obama appears to say that 'President Trump is a total and complete dipshit'. Other popular deepfakes have also drawn on skilled impersonators, such as Chris Ume's Tom Cruise videos, or clips that morph the face of comedian Bill Hader to resemble the other actors whose voices he is imitating during a TV talk show interview. The synthetic Nixon in the moon disaster video is a quite different proposition: a fully synthetic voice model of Nixon, trained on hundreds of examples of his actual voice. Respeecher's synthetic audio techniques are proprietary and the company states that it does not allow non-consensual or deceptive applications of its work. It requires written permission from living subjects who are to be revoiced, although figures of historical prominence like Nixon are treated differently. The firm's tech is marketed at films, TV, animation, games, advertising, podcasts, and audiobooks, with a significant emphasis on localizing and dubbing content into different languages while retaining the original voice. Its website includes a 'voice marketplace' in which dozens of existing voice models can be licensed for reuse.

For synthetic audio, there is an important distinction here between the creation of *text-to-speech* and *speech-to-speech* audio. Text-to-speech systems are quite familiar in a range of contexts, and various forms of read-aloud option are included as standard accessibility tools on everyday platforms and software applications. The software generates an audio version of the text, but these don't always sound very lifelike or nuanced, and can sometimes be quite robotic, with even the more elaborate versions offering only a restricted range of pre-programmed tones of voice (happy, cross, and so on). In contrast, speech-to-speech systems such as Respeecher are voice-swaps, analogous to the kinds of face-swapping processes that have characterized most of the deepfake examples discussed so far in this book. Respeecher's system trains on examples of both source and target voices until it can generate a convincing facsimile of the target voice delivering the source script: in the moon disaster example, actor Lewis Wheeler delivering the speech is output in a persuasive recreation of Richard Nixon's voice.

One example of the potential of synthetic audio is the video fronted by footballer David Beckham for the *Malaria Must Die* campaign. For this, several creative agencies including software firm Synthesia created a video of Beckham appealing to the viewer to support the campaign to eradicate malaria, in which he appears to speak in nine different languages (https://www. synthesia.io/post/david-beckham). On-screen captions tell the viewer which language Beckham's delivery has shifted into and offer English subtitles, while the voices in each case match Beckham's facial movements. The novelty of this synthetic media initiative drew a lot of attention, but it is not just a novelty. Such approaches offer enormous potential for cross-cultural communication and collaboration.

Synthetic audio offers other possibilities too. Machine learning was also used to generate a synthetic audio version of the speech that John F. Kennedy had been on his way to deliver in Dallas when he was murdered in 1963. Researchers in Edinburgh trained their system on recordings of more than 800 Kennedy speeches in order to reproduce his intonation accurately. Such synthetic audio is sometimes said to have potential for people who lose the ability to speak through illness to recover some capacity to communicate in their former voice (BBC News 2018). Project Revoice, for instance, is developing voice cloning technology for sufferers of motor neurone disease.

A more controversial synthetic audio example concerns TV chef Anthony Bourdain, who took his own life in 2018. Bourdain is the subject of a 2021 documentary feature by Morgan Neville titled *Roadrunner*. Neville had thousands of hours of video and audio recordings of Bourdain from which to compile the film, but chose to commission a synthetic audio recreation of the chef's voice to read certain lines of voiceover. These lines were words written by Bourdain for which there was no audio version (Rosner 2021). The film does not make it clear to the viewer that what they are hearing at some points in the film is not Bourdain's actual voice but a synthetic audio simulation. The effect is sufficiently convincing that there was some controversy about how much of the audio may have been synthetic, until AI startup Pindrop conducted a forensic analysis of the film's audio, identifying three short synthetic clips totalling fifty seconds (Simonite 2021).

So what counts in this example is that Neville does not let the viewer know that some of the film's audio content has been generated by AI – in essence, breaking the contract with the viewer that the rest of the documentary establishes. Compare this with the care taken in *Welcome to Chechnya* (discussed in

Chapter 3) to make the viewer understand that some figures have been digitally disguised, highlighting the distinction between reality and simulation and drawing the audience into understanding this. The very different choices made for the *Roadrunner* film point to the ways in which synthetic media can undermine or exploit their audience's trust, and in which audiences may come to feel their trust is misplaced.

There have been early examples in which synthetic audio has been used for outright deception, or in which its very existence has been used to cast doubt on the truth. For example, there are reports of fraudulent uses of such technology in commercial contexts. The CEO of one UK energy firm was fooled into transferring €220,000 to hackers who reportedly used synthetic audio techniques to imitate the voice of the boss of the German parent company (Stupp 2019). And the existence of synthetic audio technology also creates the possibility for fraudulent uses and denials in politics. Donald Trump's inauguration as US president was marked by millions of women around the world marching in protest, many wearing distinctive pink hats, to express their outrage at his attitudes towards women, captured most indelibly in an audio recording released late in the 2016 US election in which he boasted that his celebrity status allowed him to 'grab 'em by the pussy' (*New York Times* 2016). Trump acknowledged the recording was real and apologized for this at the time of its release, dismissing it as 'locker room talk', but later moved to questioning whether it was real and telling people that it wasn't his voice (Martin, Haberman & Burns 2017). Here again is Chesney and Citron's Liar's Dividend at work, where the very existence of synthetic media as a technological option is enough for the liar to cast doubt on any other piece of media. Such dilemmas have been explored in a range of deepfake art projects and information campaigns, many of which highlight dimensions of trust. The following section introduces three of these.

Reckoning with trust

'Deep Reckonings' is a conceptual art project by Stephanie Lepp. Lepp has created a series of deepfake videos in which controversial figures – all powerful men – perform public apologies for their past behaviour and promise to do better. As with Nixon, the targets are leaders with particular resources of symbolic power. At the time of writing, the series comprises five-minute deepfakes of addresses to camera by Mark Zuckerberg, Donald Trump, and US Supreme Court justice Brett Kavanaugh, whose confirmation process to the court was almost derailed by historical sexual assault claims. A fourth video shows a dialogue between libertarian podcaster Joe Rogan and *Infowars* host Alex Jones: a far-right conspiracy theorist who has been influential in promoting harmful disinformation, most notoriously the false claim that the 2012 massacre of schoolchildren at Sandy Hook Elementary School was a hoax. In each video, scripted by Lepp, these figures identify and acknowledge past wrongdoings and consider alternative futures in which they might do and be better. Her deepfake Trump monologue, for example, ends on him saying this:

> But you know what would be the most dramatic plot twist? [...] If I just acknowledged: I lost. If I did the real version of this fake-news video. If I gave the most beautiful, tremendous, perfect concession speech, in the

history of our country, the likes of which no one has ever seen.

'Deep Reckonings' is a project about trust: about how it can be lost and about what it might take to start rebuilding it. Lepp's work asks us to imagine a public sphere marked less by domination and exploitation, and more by shared openness, recognition, and contrition. The project is more than a warning about the ethical abuses that synthetic media make possible; it is explicitly about ethical abuses of various kinds, and uses synthetic media to gesture towards better futures. Lepp's work inverts the widespread anxiety about the risks of deepfakes for public trust, and instead uses them to imagine a better, more trustworthy political environment. She writes:

> The videos make their fakery explicit not only to prevent misinformation, but also to leverage a superpower of synthetic media – that we can know they're fake and they still affect us. In this spirit, Deep Reckonings explores the question: *how might we use our synthetic selves to elicit our better angels? In other words, how might we deepfake it 'til we make it?* (https://www. deepreckonings.com/about.html)

The project grew out of a thirty-episode podcast series called *Reckonings* that Lepp began in 2015. She describes the show as 'an exploration of how we change our hearts and minds'. Each episode revolves around an interview with a real individual taking stock of their lives, and recounts various epiphanies, recantations, and promised changes of direction. Episode 25, for example, features a discussion with former Facebook executive Tim Kendall. Kendall helped develop Facebook's business model of 'social advertising', in which your Facebook Friends' activities are presented to you as product recommendations, but has since become an outspoken critic of social media, which he considers addictive and harmful.

In 2019, Lepp decided to include a fictional reckoning for Pope Francis in one episode, scripting an audio recording in which a voice actor apologized for historical sexual abuse by Catholic clergy. Deepfake videos were a natural next step. Lepp's videos use a similar video dialogue replacement approach to those of Bill Posters discussed in Chapter 3. She uses voice actors to impersonate her targets, which is less expensive than creating full synthetic audio. Lepp takes great care to minimize the chances of these videos being manipulated or set in new contexts where there could be a risk of people believing them to be real. The beginnings and ends of each video include captions emphasizing they are fake, each is watermarked with the on-screen hashtag #deepreckonings, and the script of each video has its subject declare that it's a fake. (Even all this, though, may not be enough to prevent the videos being further manipulated into new contexts.)

Each video incorporates a call-to-action and urges its subject to make a real public reckoning. The scripts combine these crucial moments with the subject stating that the video is not real. The deepfake exchange between Alex Jones and Joe Rogan, for example, concludes like this:

> *Jones*: I want to pursue my original mission of seeking the truth and fighting tyranny, but I'm stuck between an audience that will literally kill me if I renege on all this stuff, and the lamestream media that won't let me change. I want to change, but I don't know how. So what do I do with this video?

Rogan: What do you mean?

Jones: Well it's fake ... but it's true.

Rogan: What if you just pretend this video is real?

Jones: That's crazy.

Rogan: You think that's crazy?! Well, what if you do the real version of this video, right here, on my show?

Jones: Hmmmm ...

'Deep Reckonings' is part of an important current in synthetic video: projects that use deepfakes of major public figures in order to warn the viewer about the dangers of deepfakes, and which situate synthetic media within a wider set of warnings about the risks to contemporary democratic systems.

Anti-corruption US pressure group RepresentUS (founded 2012) created two thirty-second deepfake political ads to air on TV during the late stages of the 2020 US presidential election. They commissioned ad agency Mischief @ No Fixed Address to create the video. The context for this was concerns over the Trump campaign's aggressive attempts to undermine postal voting, and his early indications that he would not accept a peaceful transfer of power should he lose. Trump's subsequent refusal to concede defeat and the attempted coup events at the Capitol on 6 January 2021 proved these concerns well founded.

In these TV ads, Vladimir Putin and Kim Jong-un are both made to appear to address the American people. Both deepfaked leaders are shown describing with satisfaction how it is a mistake to imagine that they are working to undermine US democracy – the American people, they say, are doing that all by themselves. Putin is made to say: 'Polling stations are closing. You are divided. You don't know who to trust. There are strings we can pull, but we don't have to. You are pulling them for us.' These deepfake ads were intended for TV broadcast in the Washington, DC, area, to air directly after one of the televised presidential debates. However, CNN, Fox, and MSNBC all dropped them shortly before they were due to screen (Hao 2020b). This was something of a test case for political synthetic media. While these videos end with a caption reading 'The footage is not real, but the threat is', there is clear potential for these videos to be misused or misunderstood if manipulated into different contexts. Here again is the paradox that raising awareness of synthetic media makes it more likely that people can exploit the Liar's Dividend.

Bill Posters, whose work we encountered in the previous chapter, has also created a project that responds to the common anxiety about deepfakes of political leaders. In 2019, Posters worked with UK-based digital rights group Future Advocacy to create a synthetic artwork called 'Partly Political Broadcasts'. The title puns on the UK genre of the party political broadcast, through which major political parties are guaranteed by law a certain amount of unpaid airtime on television in order to make direct addresses to voters. For this work, Posters created one-minute videos of both Prime Minister Boris Johnson and then-Leader of the Opposition Jeremy Corbyn that were released during that year's general election campaign. Rather than addressing the nation and asking for support in the election, each leader is instead made to endorse their opponent. The videos were designed to complement Future Advocacy's push for synthetic media regulation and greater public understanding of their uses – what we could call synthetic media literacy.

The videos were a direct response to the media attention received by Posters' earlier Zuckerberg video and the tone of its coverage as a threat to democracy. 'Partly Political Broadcasts' was at the same time a warning about the disinformation possibilities of synthetic media and a playful celebration of the possibilities of synthetic art. This is the text of the Boris Johnson video, which parodies his fondness for dropping Latin tags and classical allusions into public speech, as well as referencing an infamous video of Johnson steamrollering a small child in a photo-op rugby game:

> Hi folks, I am here with a very special message. Since that momentous day in 2016, division has coursed through our country as we argue with fantastic passion, vim and vigour about Brexit. My friends, I wish to rise above this divide and endorse my worthy opponent, the Right Honourable Jeremy Corbyn, to be Prime Minister of our United Kingdom. Only he, not I, can make Britain great again. Huzza! Alas, why should you believe me? Much like Odysseus and his encounter with the cyclops Polyphemus, I too am nobody. I am a fake. A deepfake, to be precise. And as you can see, even I, the Prime Minister, can be affected by them. The unregulated power of technologies like this risks fuelling misinformation, eroding trust and compromising democracy. Help us rugby-tackle deepfakes, not children, at futureadvocacy. org/deepfakes. *Castigat ridendo mores.*

As with Lepp's 'Deep Reckonings', the script explicitly acknowledges the deepfake nature of the video in an attempt to minimize potential harms from its being manipulated into new contexts. The project team worked with BBC journalists to reduce the risks of circulating these parodies during a live election campaign. Both videos were released simultaneously on social media and on BBC news, where the context made it clear that they were satirical artworks rather than actual disinformation. Both videos point out that if the biometric facial data of the UK's two most senior politicians can be appropriated in this way, then such loss of control of one's image could happen to anyone.

Posters (2021a) describes these works as examples of *détournement*. This was the Situationist tactic that sought to interrupt flows of meanings in order to create moments of opportunity for people to rethink (Debord & Wolman 2009 [1956]). *Détournement* describes creative, activist tactics that would today be described as media remix and manipulation. It describes editing texts and editing contexts in order to draw attention to both the original meanings and their suggested juxtapositions: 'a politics of subversive quotation', as Greil Marcus has it (1989: 179), and a 'reversal of perspective', in Raoul Vaneigem's words (1983 [1967]: 144). In Guy Debord's work, *détournement* was a tactic to undermine what he called the *spectacle*, a still very contemporary cultural condition characterized by 'incessant technological renewal; integration of state and economy; generalised secrecy; unanswerable lies; an eternal present' (1990: 11–12). This found resonance in later practices such as culture jamming, in which Posters has a history of creative activity. Culture jamming belongs above all to a late twentieth-century historical moment in which the emergence of networked digital media offered possible alternatives to the hierarchical relations of meaning offered by the dominant media systems. The signature gesture was to take a familiar sign and refashion it as a question mark (Meikle 2002, 2007). But in the very different media environment of the 2020s, it's no longer clear that setting out to jam an audience's perceptions, or to deliberately confuse and mislead in the name of media literacy, is a tactic best suited to the problems of the time.

Manipulating machineries of trust

In March 2022, a deepfake video of Ukrainian president Volodymyr Zelensky, in which he appeared to order his forces to surrender to the Russian invaders, was uploaded to YouTube, Facebook, and Russian social media platform VKontakte, as well as circulating on Telegram. A Ukrainian TV channel also reported that its website had been hacked, with the intruders inserting stills from the fake video and tampering with its scrolling updates (Giansiracusa 2022; Simonite 2022; Wakefield 2022). The video is unconvincing – the fake Zelensky's head doesn't match the body – but high production values are not always necessary for propaganda, and in a volatile crisis some people seeing such a news clip on their phones could have been taken in. In this instance, because pro-Russia disinformation efforts had been anticipated, Zelensky and the media were ready and able to respond. The Ukrainian leader issued an immediate video rebuttal, the TV channel was quick to declare it had been hacked, and key social media platforms announced they had removed the video. But this careful and united response in fact underlines the risks of deceptive synthetic media in other contexts where less-prepared protagonists could be taken more by surprise.

This example highlights some of the problems of interpretation, meaning, and trust that have special resonance for our understandings of news. News is a collaborative process of making meanings from events. The news is a representation of social authority, and tries to define reality for its users, viewers, and readers (Carey 1989). So news media have developed particular machineries of trust: their self-appointed role as the Fourth Estate, the unelected guarantors of democracy; their particular genres of saying and showing; their focus on high-status official sources of information; their public mantras of balance and objectivity (Curran & Seaton 2018). There is the imprimatur and the brand of the news organization, sometimes developed over one or even two centuries. There is the visual grammar of the broadcast report: the authority of the presenters; the presence of reporters at every scene; the visual evidence given for every story; the use of visuals and graphics to convey technical information. There is the reliance upon expert or hierarchically powerful sources, and the claim to eschew opinion and bias. There is the use of story-telling conventions that the audience has absorbed over many years. All of these are mechanisms deployed to present authority and invite trust. Each of these is challenged by deepfakes.

Deepfakes arrive in a context in which those machineries of trust are being widely manipulated and subverted. The authority of the news organization or brand may be a less reliable pillar than before if the source of what we encounter on our social media feeds is no longer always certain. Those news institutions and organizations are also changing in response to external and internal forces: BBC News, for example, is not what it was before the EU referendum, as the reshaping of British political discourses around questions of national identity has stretched its conventions of balance beyond their limits. Bad actors, some of them leaders of developed nations, have learned that the media's machineries of trust can be easily distorted. The news is a hierarchy machine, so high-status individuals can have their statements presented without comment. And TV needs images, so politicians supply them. These too will be presented without comment. The machineries of trust themselves are built on trust: media organizations must trust the subjects of the news to approach the arena in good faith, to observe the rules around which the media have designed their game. This is visibly no longer happening in many cases and the news has not found ways to respond.

What was demonstrated in the 2020 US presidential election and the assault on the Capitol in January 2021 – which the US Senate Committee on the Judiciary described as 'a violent attempt to subvert democracy' (2021: 6) – was that democracy can be undermined and imperilled without synthetic media. This stalled Trump putsch has left the US with many millions of voters who believe his Big Lie that the election was stolen from them. Trump presents the entire electoral process and the election itself as fake, and asks his supporters to trust him on this. Elaborate deepfakes just weren't necessary when the sitting president had access to Twitter and Facebook, and had compliant client media at Fox.

So-called *fake news* is a problematic label. One problem is that the term tries to combine a very wide range of different phenomena. It covers satire and parody, but also organized disinformation campaigns by state actors. It covers attempts to make money by gaming social media algorithms for clicks, but also the rapid spread of mistaken reports in a frenzied hashtag. That's a lot of conceptual heavy lifting for a single term. Another problem is the way that *fake news* was weaponized by Donald Trump as a way of dismissing legitimate but unfavourable coverage of his presidency, a tactic that others were quick to adopt. As Alice

Marwick and Rebecca Lewis point out, the irony of this is that the very term *fake news* itself became a tool of disinformation (2017: 44). So as an analytical tool, *fake news* lacks precision. But it does mark out a broad field of concerns, each of which can perhaps better be understood by comparison with the others, and each of which can then be explored with more specific concepts and vocabulary – the same, of course, is true of the term *deepfake*.

Photoshop disasters

Media manipulation is not new. There are long prehistories and many antecedents to today's anxieties over deepfakes. Take photography. There is a sense in which all photographs are manipulated, insofar as they are a framed and mediated representation of the world. These processes of framing and representation involve numerous choices and technical interventions (focus, flash, filter) that can be thought of as manipulating the image. We are surrounded by manipulated digital images, and we manipulate images ourselves in turn: cropping, retouching, and running them through filters, before posting them online where others too may manipulate them further. As Mia Fineman points out in her catalogue that accompanied a major exhibition of photographic manipulation at New York's Metropolitan Museum of Art, the decades since the first release of Photoshop in 1990, and the rise of ubiquitous digital photography in the smartphone era, have brought with them 'a heightened awareness of the malleability of the photographic image and a corresponding loss of faith in photography as an accurate, trustworthy means of representing the visible world' (2012: 4).

Fineman suggests that a manipulated image is one in which 'the final image is not identical to what the camera "saw" in the instant at which the negative was exposed' (2012: 7). She argues that photographic manipulation is as old as photography itself:

Nearly every kind of manipulation we now associate with Photoshop was also part of photography's predigital repertoire, from slimming waistlines and smoothing away wrinkles to adding people to (or removing them from) pictures, changing backgrounds, and fabricating events that never actually took place. (2012: 5)

The history of in-camera effects and post-production techniques – multiple exposures, photomontage, airbrushing – constitute what Fineman calls 'a secret history of photography as a medium of fabricated truth and artful lies' (2012: 6). Photography, as Nathan Jurgenson puts it, has always been 'a game of metaphor' (2019: 94).

Manipulating images of political events and leaders has a long history. The Paris Commune of 1871 was recorded in a widely distributed series of distorted and doctored photographs (early collages) designed to undermine the public perception of the Communards (Fineman 2012: 95). Staged propaganda photographs promoted nationalist sentiments in the First World War. The photomontages of the Berlin Dada group developed a new vocabulary for political commentary derived from cutting up and juxtaposing photographic images. Stalin's USSR made extensive use for decades of wholesale photo editing and manipulation to give increased prominence to political figures or to remove them from the record altogether (Fineman 2012: 89–91). Fineman writes: 'The temptation to "rectify" photographic documents has proved irresistible to modern demagogues of all stripes, from Adolf Hitler to Mao Zedong to Joseph McCarthy' (2012: 91).

For a more contemporary example, we might recall that the first day of Donald Trump's term in office was marked by his press spokesman Sean Spicer arguing with reporters about photos of the size of the crowd at the presidential inauguration. Images released by the Trump White House were markedly different from those released by other organizations, including the US National Park Service, which administers the space in which the inauguration was held. Freedom of Information requests filed by reporters at the *Guardian* later found evidence of behind-the-scenes demands for photos that were more flattering to the president. Official images cropped out the large swathes of empty space in the thin crowd on the National Mall, in an attempt to make them compare more favourably with the far larger crowds at the first inauguration of Trump's predecessor, Barack Obama (Swaine 2018).

Manipulating texts, manipulating contexts

So image manipulation is not a new phenomenon or even a distinctively digital one. And it is certainly not confined to synthetic media. It can take a wide range of different forms, between which it's useful to distinguish before we turn to our final set of examples. In Chapter 3, I used a distinction between *remixing texts* and *remixing contexts*. The same distinction is useful here in approaching misinformation and disinformation, except that in this chapter I use the word *manipulate* instead of the word *remix*. This is to enable some space and some difference between projects with creative or pro-social intentions or potential (*remix*) and those with more malign intentions or potential (*manipulate*). In both cases, we are talking about practices of creating with found material, about practices of cultural dialogue and exchange, about practices of engagement with established cultural and media forms. The actual practices can overlap and blur. The distinction I try to maintain is at the level of apparent intent and evident outcome.

Misinformation, for example, can be distinguished from *disinformation* at the level of intent. The *mis* in misinformation is related to those in *misspeak*, *misstep*, *mistake*: someone somewhere has just got something wrong. There may be consequences, as the misinformation spreads from one context to another, but the initial intention was not to deceive. The imperative for *speed* in news is a significant factor in the spread of misinformation in the social media era. But the *dis* in disinformation is related to those in *disturb* or *disrupt*. This time, someone somewhere knows exactly what they're doing, and the initial intent is very much to deceive (for more on this distinction between misinformation and disinformation, see Jack 2017 and Wardle 2020).

So we might encounter examples of *manipulated texts*: images, audio, and video that have been cropped or clipped or spliced, slowed down or sped up, or had their quality altered through post-production manipulation of lighting, framing, colour, or general quality. And we might encounter examples of *manipulated contexts*: authentic images or videos presented in a misleading context. In its free online training course for journalists 'Identifying and Tackling Manipulated Media', Reuters reports that this is the most common manipulation encountered in newsrooms. Manipulated contexts might involve images that deliberately or inadvertently omit or distort the context of an event. Or that context may have just been misunderstood, so that reporters risk using authentic imagery to present a mistaken impression. Or it may be a deliberate choice, with an image from one situation being falsely used to suggest something about another (Reuters News Agency 2019; see also Marwick & Lewis 2017; Wardle 2020).

Although the 2020 US presidential election had appeared a very likely target for significant deepfake activity, the most consequential interventions have all appeared in this book already, from the slowed-down video of Nancy Pelosi discussed in Chapter 1, to the pro-democracy advocacy videos of RepresentUS discussed above. Deepfake monitoring firm Sensity reported in March 2021 that:

> Despite experts' predictions, deepfakes did not have any tangible impact either on the US Presidential Election in 2020, nor on any other global political events of the year. To the best of our knowledge, no bad actors, either independent or state-sponsored, have made use of deepfake videos or audio for spreading disinformation or political propaganda. (Patrini 2021: 3)

Sensity also noted that the only significant exception to this was the very widespread use of fake photos generated by synthetic media, of the kind produced by the This Person Does Not Exist website discussed in Chapter 1. Their report notes that such images are widely used all over the internet in the creation of bots and fake profiles on social media (Patrini 2021: 3). For an idea of the scale of such fake profiles, Twitter's annual report for 2021 estimated that around 5% of their regular daily users were fake accounts or bots, and acknowledged that this estimate could be on the low side (Twitter, Inc. 2022: 5). As Twitter claimed 217 million 'monetizable daily active users' by December 2021 (Twitter, Inc. 2022: 40), that's a cautious estimate of almost 11 million active bots and fake accounts. For the same period, Meta's internal monitoring of their Facebook, Instagram, Messenger, and WhatsApp platforms estimated 3% of their total 'monthly active people' (MAP) to be fake accounts (Meta Platforms, Inc. 2022: 5). Each of these platforms is a great deal larger than Twitter, with a combined total of 3.59 billion MAP as of December 2021 (2022: 50), so in this case the figure of 3% is about 108 million accounts dedicated to potentially misleading, deceptive, or fraudulent activity.

This last section of the chapter draws on three examples of contemporary political media manipulation. Each revolves around a claim that someone's political opponents are using deepfakes to undermine them. In each, there are questions of manipulated texts and manipulated contexts. And in each case, it's far from certain that any deepfakes are actually involved.

The first example involved President Ali Bongo of Gabon. Bongo had disappeared from public view for several months before his government posted a video of the president sending a New Year message to the country. To many in Gabon, including some prominent opposition politicians, the video didn't look right, with the president's facial expressions unlike his usual appearance. Rumours spread that the video was a deepfake, made to suppress the fact that Bongo was dead or incapacitated. These rumours led within days to an attempted military coup. Bongo later reappeared, and it emerged that he had suffered a stroke in August 2018, the effects of which explained his changed appearance in the video (Ajder et al. 2019: 10). The *Washington Post* commissioned two sets of forensic examinations of the video, neither of which found any evidence of synthetic media (Cahlan 2020). This example shows the *illusion* of a deepfake being used to fuel a volatile political situation. What counts here is that deepfakes just exist. In this case, this simple fact is enough to destabilize a political situation without any actual deepfake videos being involved. This is perhaps the greatest risk of deepfakes for political communication and public trust.

The second example involves a political controversy that developed in Myanmar in 2021 around a video that depicted a high-ranking politician, Phyo Min Thein, appearing to confess to corruption charges that implicated the country's former leader Aung San Suu Kyi. Many suspected the video was a deepfake, pointing to some odd glitches and bad syncing, and to the subject's strained voice. Some social media users circulated images of screenshots claiming to show the results of deepfake detection algorithms proving the video was fake (Gregory 2021b). Others noted that the quality of this online video was already low enough for the glitches to be simple compression artefacts. So was this a fake video designed to undermine one faction in Myanmar's politics? Or, as suggested by deepfakes expert Sam Gregory (2021b) of international human rights organization WITNESS, was it the rather more familiar genre of the coerced confession? (And whether it was a deepfake or a forced confession, either one meant making the speaker say things they otherwise would not.) Here again, controversy is caused not by the clear use of a deepfake but rather by the apparent potential for this.

A key issue here is that of *context collapse*: the ways in which the sharing of content across networked digital media strips any text of its context, and the challenges this creates for individuals. The concept of context collapse has been central to the study of social media since their inception (Wesch 2009; boyd 2014), and is relevant to our third example. In June 2019, a video circulated widely in Malaysia purporting to be a sex tape involving government minister Azmin Ali and another man, political staffer Haziq Abdul Aziz. Homosexuality is illegal in Malaysia and there is a history of political scandal around gay sex, including a long-running case involving former deputy prime minister Anwar Ibrahim. The second man in the Ali tape stated it was a real sex tape, whereas Ali and the country's prime minister claimed it was a deepfake. As with the Gabon example, forensic examination found no evidence of synthetic media (Ajder et al. 2019: 10). To complicate the picture further, some claimed that the video in which Haziq confessed to appearing in the sex tape was itself a deepfake (Golingai 2019). So was the sex video real and was Ali exploiting the Liar's Dividend of deepfakes to make people doubt the truth? Or was that video real but Ali not the man on screen? Or was the video actually synthetic and being used to destabilize the government? And what about the second video, in which Haziq confesses to being one of the men in the sex tape: was *that* a deepfake, as some suggested? Such questions would be difficult to answer in a courtroom. But when they cascade across WhatsApp and Twitter, gaining and losing contexts and comments as they move, they become combustible material whether there is an actual deepfake in the story or not.

Summary

Deepfakes are about communication. They are about new ways of making meanings and they challenge our understandings of how meanings get made. If trust is central to the making of meanings, then it is central to an analysis of deepfakes too. The examples discussed in detail in this chapter are deepfake texts in which concepts of trust resonate: 'In Event of Moon Disaster' with its subversion of the presidential TV address, or 'Deep Reckonings' with its alternative realities in which public figures seek to regain the public's trust. The very existence of deepfakes is a destabilizing moment for concepts of trust in public communication. The uses of synthetic images in fake profile photos and of synthetic audio in all kinds of contexts are increasing. The more people become aware of and educated about these phenomena, the easier it may be to denounce any real piece of media as fake: the Liar's Dividend (Chesney & Citron 2019). This is the dynamic in play in the examples from Gabon, Myanmar, and Malaysia: not so much bad actors creating deepfake texts to destabilize democracy, but rather a range of actors invoking the *possibility* of deepfake texts in order to corrode public trust.

Deepfakes are a social media artefact: from the ways that machine-learning researchers have drawn upon social media data to train their models, to the ways that the algorithmic architectures of key platforms allow the circulation of distorted content, deepfakes are not a coincidence with social media but are intrinsic to those media. Deepfakes help to reveal the reality of what social media are. They are part of a coming wave of synthetic content for which we are in many ways unprepared: the media machineries of trust I have discussed in this chapter are not necessarily adequate to the task of responding to synthetic media. The greatest risk of deepfakes in these contexts of political communication may simply be that they are known to exist: if we know

145

that everything can be faked, we risk losing the capacity to believe in anything. This would be different from a literate scepticism about potentially partisan claims. It would be a destabilizing of the entire scaffolding of public communication on which democracy depends.

Conclusion

This book began with the idea that communication is the making of meanings. So what final meanings for now can we make from deepfakes? What does it mean that synthetic media are emerging so rapidly, and converging with other forms of manipulated and remixed media? If communication is the making of meanings, and involves the creation, distribution, and interpretation of messages, I want to extend that here to say that technology is also communication. In the forms of technological objects and systems, there are also messages being exchanged and meanings produced. (This also locates technology firmly at the centre of the study of communication and media.) There are messages being produced, encoded, and sent in the development and shaping, in the adoption and adaptation, of technological innovations. There are messages encoded into technologies themselves: the unauthorized app that your iPhone won't let you install, for instance, embodies certain political relationships, certain views about intellectual property and commercial exchange. And meanings are also being produced at the receiving end as users interpret and make sense of technologies:

147

sometimes in their adoption or rejection, sometimes in their adaptation or transformation. Technology is communication. So what meanings are we to make of the new technologies of deepfakes? Why do deepfakes matter?

One reason they matter is that deepfakes are a part of the larger category of synthetic media, media that are created or altered using AI techniques. AI is the contested site of countless bids for power. AI describes the industries that are growing up to use specific applications, but it also describes a specialist field of computer science. And AI is also a magnetic focus of fantasies and wishes, where science fiction meets venture capital, and it is a significant generator of marketing hype and futurist vapourware. In this book, I have tried to avoid speculation or writing in the future tense, but it seems clear that at least in the short term, while the hype cycles of AI and machine learning are still running, the possibilities of synthetic media will continue to draw experimentation, creativity, and abuse before they become taken for granted. Synthetic images, audio, and video will find new applications, and will be adopted and adapted in ways we may not yet have imagined, far less covered in this book. Their uses and abuses will shape how they are developed, and whether the new uses to which they are put are integrated into our daily lives or rejected. Some of these uses may be exciting, educational, and creative, but others may be repressive, exploitative, and abusive.

I don't mean to suggest here that synthetic media are somehow neutral, with potential for good or bad, and that it just depends what we do with them: that is a naïve response to any technology. Instead, I mean to suggest that technologies develop through a kind of contest between contending social groups and actors.

148

Conclusion

The interests of researchers, designers, and developers are not always the same as the interests of end users, manufacturers, governments, and regulators, and in the processes of adoption and adaptation that all of these actors are involved in lie the moments of stability that we come to think of as technologies (Meikle & Young 2012). The things themselves also matter, and also have a role in these processes (Latour 1991). As Langdon Winner argues: 'The things we call "technologies" are ways of building order in our world' (1986: 28). We've seen in this book that the enormous datasets used to train machine-learning systems to generate, remix, and manipulate human images have drawn upon sources of data that may be considered exploitation or even piracy. Algorithms are social: they embody real human, social relationships, and those relationships involve power, winners and losers. How these systems are programmed to run, the data they are given to work with, and how the results are encountered in the world – all of these are social and political questions, not just things to be left to the maths experts.

Deepfakes are an example of such processes of technological emergence, and they illustrate how technologies are material expressions of social relations. Is it pure chance that their dominant use to date has been in the creation of non-consensual pornographic videos of women? Or does that instead tell us things about the kinds of society in which that use can so easily become established as the standard application for a new medium of visual communication? The historical moment in which they emerge is also not coincidental, but rather it is fundamental to deepfakes that they emerge in the social media era. I have argued in this book that deepfakes are part of the social media environment, not just something random happening at

149

the same time. Deepfakes are in part a consequence of the enormous availability of images that has been driven by social media and digital firms. And deepfakes are very much a product of the social media worldview in which all human experience is just there to be mediated without the need for any meaningful or informed consent. First they took our address books, then they took our daily step-counts, and now our very faces are the raw material for more digital extraction. At what point will we say no?

So one more reason why deepfakes matter is that they are a new marker in our experiences of digital exploitation. At a certain point, we will have to stop allowing the collection and manipulation of our personal data by any chancer who happens across them. Perhaps it is already too late, as the data are largely already out there and have already been fed into neural networks, used to train systems that can be deployed in as yet unimagined ways. But we should make it clear that our consent is not being given and that this matters. I don't just mean some *quit Facebook!* form of response that depends on billions of individuals all taking the same action. Rather, I mean there is a need for regulation.

Regulation doesn't only come in the form of laws. In a very useful analysis of what other forces can enable or constrain behaviour, Lawrence Lessig (1999) points also to the operations of the marketplace, the architecture of a space or system (including software code), and the acceptable limits of social norms. Each of these can independently influence people's behaviour, and they can also be seen as interdependent. One of Lessig's key examples of this is the regulation of smoking. Smoking is constrained in certain circumstances by laws: it's illegal to smoke in restaurants or on trains where I live, and may well be illegal where you live too. But the marketplace can also be used to influence people's smoking behaviour: taxes can be raised on cigarettes to the point where people feel the need to quit (an indirect use of law), and the range of choice or price of available cigarettes can also either constrain or enable people's behaviour. The architecture of a cigarette could also be changed, altering the levels of nicotine to make it less addictive or of other chemicals to make it less carcinogenic. And the social norms around smoking have changed enormously in the past couple of decades, with smoking seen as increasingly unacceptable in more and more social contexts (Lessig 1999: 120–37). All of these forces together – laws, the market, architecture, and social norms – have driven smoking in many countries to far lower levels than was the case twenty or thirty years ago.

So in thinking about how deceptive or abusive synthetic and manipulated media might be regulated, we can think about all of these same forces as possibilities. These final pages suggest some ways that law, the market, software code, and social norms might all offer ways of responding to the problems of exploitative or manipulative synthetic media, without inhibiting their potential creative or educational uses: the Salvador Dalí deepfake we encountered in Chapter 3, for instance, is a very different use of synthetic media from the faked Emma Watson porn videos we encountered in Chapter 2, so it's important to keep such distinctions in mind when thinking about regulation.

Legal mechanisms

The first of Lessig's kinds of regulation is law. Concerns around disinformation and around non-consensual sexual imagery are being expressed in legal responses in many parts of the world. Chesney and Citron's important 2019 overview of the challenges and threats of deepfake technologies identifies a very wide range of legal dilemmas and risks to individuals, communities, and nation-states, from missed employment opportunities to military conflict, and canvasses a correspondingly wide range of potential remedies and strategies for mitigation. To focus on one example from the UK, the government published proposed legislation on regulating online harms in May 2021. This proposal illustrates some of the difficulties of regulating content while also pointing to some of the possibilities of requiring tech platforms to change their algorithms. While this Draft Online Safety Bill does not mention deepfakes, synthetic media, or AI by name, it does propose to give UK media regulator Ofcom more powers to act in relation to websites that host potentially harmful content, even if that content is otherwise legal; anti-vaccination disinformation is specified as an example in an accompanying briefing paper from the House of Commons Library (Woodhouse 2021). Platforms that facilitate the sharing of legal-but-harmful user-generated content, from Facebook to MrDeepFakes, would be liable to fines of up to 10% of annual global turnover if these proposals were to become law. Journalism and users' comments on journalism are specifically excluded, but not clearly defined. At the time of writing in April 2022, the legislation has still not passed, in part due to the very real conceptual difficulties of identifying legal-but-harmful content while not at the same time impinging on free speech and expression. Whether it ever passes into law or not, this contested proposal stands as an example of the complexities of regulating algorithmic media systems.

Conclusion

One significant aspect of this proposed legislation is that it specifies that one factor in determining possible harm of various kinds is the 'algorithms used by the service, and how easily, quickly and widely content may be disseminated by means of the service' (Draft Online Safety Bill 2021: 6–8). So the focus is not just on the kinds of content shared, which is one root of the concerns about free speech, but also on the algorithmic operations of platforms. This is an important dimension to any response to problematic deepfake content of the kinds discussed particularly in Chapter 2 of this book. Algorithmic sharing, visible engagement metrics, behavioural advertising, targeted personalized content – deepfakes are not a mutation from these strategies. They are one logical outcome of those strategies. These practices create a system that more or less demands to find expression in manipulated media content.

Visible engagement metrics, for example, are not just about counting numbers of *likes* or *shares*. They are ways that social media platforms try to shape our responses to content, through the options to *like* and *share* rather than, say, to *hate* or *vaporize*. Karin Wahl-Jorgensen (2019) argues that the range of responses offered by Facebook's reaction emojis represents a deliberate curating of our emotional responses to what we encounter on the site. For commercial reasons, Facebook encodes a specific and restricted range of emotional responses as tools for measuring user engagement, in order to market this data to advertisers. So if we are disturbed by the potential that networked digital media bring for the creation and distribution of deepfakes, then we need to rethink what we allow social media companies to do, including automated sharing and the measurement and display of people's responses to content. This is not an argument for censorship or an attack on free speech. Regulating the algorithmic circulation of messages that are being shared for corporate profit is not the same thing as regulating speech.

Social media are principal vectors for the circulation of manipulated media. Personalized advertising based on our data histories, automated sharing, and non-transparent algorithmic operations should all be regulated, either by the platforms themselves or by law if necessary. A key consideration here is that the algorithms used to curate and order social media feeds are not transparent to the user. It should always be clear to the user exactly why they are seeing a particular link or image or post. For example, Instagram used to be organized around a time-based feed that displayed posts in reverse chronological order, so that the most recent post appeared at the top. That was a form of algorithmic sorting, but the user could recognize and understand what the sorting process was. But when Instagram changed to a more complex and less transparent set of algorithms that selected content based on perceived relevance and interest to the user, then the user lost the ability to understand why they were seeing this post and not that one (Leaver, Highfield & Abidin 2020: 18–20). Facebook also imposed a move from 'most recent' to 'top stories': researcher Elinor Carmi recorded the platform changing her newsfeed preferences to 'top stories' against her wishes seventy-one times in one year (2020: 207). The user should always be able to see why a post is in their feed, and should have some control over this. This becomes important as misleading manipulated and synthetic media circulate across social media platforms.

A related problem here is the use of engagement metrics as part of social media platforms' business models. Posts that have been *liked* and *shared* thousands of times gather more *likes* and *shares*, like snowballs tumbling down a hill. This evidence of apparent popularity can confer a certain legitimacy on a post: *everyone else is sharing this, so there must be something in it.* But recall the example from Chapter 1 of the deceptive, manipulated Nancy Pelosi video that was shared more than 90,000 times, and of Facebook's dismal labelling of it as 'partly false'. If the numbers of *shares* and *likes* on such content were visible only to the original poster, then deceptive synthetic or manipulated media might not find such easy traction. Instagram, for one, has experimented with hiding users' *like* counts in various countries since 2019 in an attempt to reduce social and peer pressure on younger people in particular (BBC News 2019; Ribeiro 2019). But this has so far been a messy and uneven process. Depending where and when you read this, a post you see on Instagram might variously indicate *175,520 likes*, or *Liked by [an account you follow closely]*, or nothing at all. As the ongoing development of this Instagram policy appears driven by the commercial needs of advertisers, marketers, and influencers, it offers a dispiriting example to anyone concerned about the role of engagement metrics in encouraging the circulation of deceptive synthetic or manipulated media. So if restricting the visibility of engagement metrics is inimical to the advertising business models of the biggest social media platforms, then they may need a legal push.

In one of its frequent periods of public damage control, Facebook announced in November 2021 that it was changing its use of facial recognition technologies. As mentioned in Chapter 1, Facebook's model DeepFace was originally trained on 4 million images of Facebook users (Raji & Fried 2021: 3), and was used to automatically tag people when another user uploaded their picture. Facebook said it would delete the facial recognition templates that DeepFace had scanned from users' photos. This would affect *more than 1 billion people*, a third of the platform's 3 billion daily users, or about one in eight of everyone alive. Facebook's vice-president for AI wrote: 'We need to weigh the positive use cases for facial recognition against growing societal concerns, especially as regulators have yet to provide clear rules' (Pesenti 2021). On one level, this is welcome recognition that those 'growing societal concerns' are real and valid. For example, as noted in Chapter 1, other companies have built their own machine-learning models by harvesting people's pictures from platforms such as Facebook. But on another level, this is evasive language, blaming a lack of regulation for the company's own choices and practices. And Facebook did not say that it would be deleting the DeepFace model itself, which it instead retains and can continue to refine for likely future use.

Market mechanisms

What of the next of Lessig's categories, using market mechanisms to regulate the problematic forms of deepfake media? Chapter 2 of this book began by citing figures published by Pornhub, in which that platform boasted about its users' enormous numbers of searches for celebrity sex videos. It was revealing that Pornhub actually trumpeted these celebrity porn search statistics *in a media release*, despite the transparent problems with that content. As *Vice* journalist Samantha Cole (2020b) pointed out, Pornhub had banned the search term *deepfakes* in 2018, but was still hosting and monetizing large numbers of synthetic videos that didn't use the actual word *deepfake* in their descriptions.

But an important turning point in Pornhub's approach to non-consensual content came in December 2020, when the *New York Times* published a long investigation into underage abuse videos on that platform (Kristof 2020). It interviewed numerous women whose sexual assaults had been uploaded to Pornhub. These women described how the videos continued to haunt them years later, as they would be reuploaded every time they succeeded in having them removed. The issue in this event was not deepfakes, but real abuse videos. At that time, Pornhub was claiming 3.5 billion monthly visits, which, according to the *New York Times*, was more than Amazon or Netflix. Visa and Mastercard responded to the *New York Times* piece by announcing that they would no longer process transactions on Pornhub, following the same move previously taken by PayPal.

So faced with this market sanction, overnight, Pornhub removed 9 million of its 13 million videos, taking down everything that was not uploaded by a 'verified' user (Paul 2020). We should note that a 'verified user' is one who has sent Pornhub a picture of themselves holding up a sign with their username and the name of the site written on it – a process that suggests hostage-taking more than consent. (For a different interpretation, see van der Nagel 2020, who examines the same process on Reddit's /r/gonewild forum as a technology of explicit consent.) Some might pause at the prospect of a society where Mastercard sets the limits of public discourse or where Visa awards itself the role of chief censor. But neither of those companies had in fact demanded Pornhub remove any content – they simply declined to process its payments. It was Pornhub itself that decided the solution was deleting most of its catalogue. In this one event, non-consensual sexual videos on commercial websites were revealed to be in part a commercial problem that could be tackled in part with commercial solutions. Not all sites are as vulnerable to such action as Pornhub: other payment options, including Patreon or bank transfers, remain viable, and MrDeepFakes runs on cryptocurrencies, not Mastercard. But crypto-currency providers have also introduced sanctions in some cases. Coinbase, for example, are reported to have suspended the payment account of DeepSukebe in 2021, after the site had received critical media attention (see Burgess 2021; Cook 2021; Wakefield 2021).

Deepfake detection systems

As well as laws and market mechanisms, Lessig shows how changes to the architecture or code of a system can act as a form of regulation. Changes to a technology can work to constrain or to enable particular kinds of behaviour. Some are working to identify algorithmic manipulation through algorithmic detection methods. A consortium of industry and academic researchers, including Facebook and Microsoft, launched a Deepfake Detection Challenge contest in 2019 that drew over 2,000 entrants (Meta AI 2020). Some such systems work to detect artefacts or anomalies in videos that are more easily identified by machines than by humans (Mirsky & Lee 2020). But such technical models for detecting deepfakes risk falling into a kind of arms race, constantly playing catch-up with improvements in deepfake production. A relevant irony here is that, as we saw in Chapter 1, a process of enhanced deception is intrinsic to creating deepfakes. The production of such synthetic media in fact works through systems responding to detection by competing neural networks, and adapting to produce more believable images.

One more promising area in which this is being explored for problematic uses of synthetic media is with the development of technologies of tracing and trust: *content authenticity* or *content provenance* approaches that embed traceable histories for the authentication of images and video. This could involve manufacturers adding tamper-proof metadata to software used in image and video editing, or enabling digital watermarks that are visible to machines but not to the human viewer. Manipulated content could then be debunked by tracing it to its origins, while authentic content could be verified: something that could be important, to take one example, in documenting human rights abuses.

It's not hard to imagine privacy and surveillance risks to making media in certain contexts verifiably traceable to a specific individual or device. And such systems could inadvertently undermine the credibility of real images that are created outside those systems. But the overall push towards authenticatable content has a lot of promise. Human rights group WITNESS has been a leader in driving and debating these approaches (and in driving public awareness of deepfakes in general), and has excellent resources on its website and its YouTube channel for readers who would like to explore this further. One significant collaboration in this area is the Content Authenticity Initiative, in which Adobe, Microsoft, WITNESS, the BBC, Twitter, the *New York Times*, and others are working to develop industry standards for authentication of images and videos.

This kind of forensic approach is not one for non-professional individuals online to use when encountering something weird on their daily timelines, but could be employed by newsrooms, by content creators, and by organizations working to try to limit the damage caused by manipulated media in a particular event. More user-friendly kinds of code approach could involve persuading closed messaging apps such as WhatsApp to add some kind of *is this real?* button which users could click to have the app check the integrity of an image or video that is circulating in their community. One more would be the accelerated development and availability of reverse-video-search tools that enable users to check for themselves if something seems too good or too bad to be true (WITNESS 2018).

Synthetic media literacy

Such proposals connect with questions of synthetic media literacy, which I use here in relation to Lessig's fourth modality of regulation, that of changing social norms. Changing norms can be illustrated here by the young people whom we saw in Chapter 1 chanting 'fuck the algorithm'. We may mistrust algorithmic systems, but we can sometimes choose to reject them too – and in that case, the public outcry about those changes to school qualifications forced the UK government into a U-turn. This example suggests a shifting social norm, an indication of where one limit to the acceptable now lies. Such boundaries move, but may sometimes need a push. To draw upon Langdon Winner again: 'In an age in which the inexhaustible power of scientific technology makes all things possible, it remains to be seen where we will draw the line, where we will be able to say, here are possibilities that wisdom suggests we avoid' (1986: xi).

Understanding how and where to draw such lines in this case requires better public understanding of deepfakes, and better understanding of them by news organizations and politicians in particular. This doesn't mean expecting everyone to turn into a deepfake forensics expert. Rather it means that the real responsibility for deeper understanding of synthetic media should be pushed upstream to journalists, regulators, and social media platforms, all of whom are in more powerful positions to take meaningful action against deepfakes than are general publics: the free online Reuters training course for journalists mentioned in Chapter 4 is a strong initiative in this direction (Reuters News Agency 2019). At the same time, it does also mean that those general publics should have a better understanding of how content is produced and circulated in today's networked digital media environment, and of the roles of algorithms in determining what they see and what they don't.

Media literacy is sometimes seen as a soft option compared to the heavy lifting of regulating media industries. But up-to-date digital media literacy is essential in understanding how synthetic, manipulated, and remixed media can be created and circulated. The challenge is to do this without encouraging kneejerk cynicism or a disabling scepticism. We need to avoid the trap of dismissing everything as potentially fake just because we know there is the possibility that sometimes some things might be. The Liar's Dividend is a very real threat, and can certainly be exploited more easily, frequently, and quickly than persuasive deepfakes can be made.

The shift in social norms that could really help against malicious deepfakes is one that rethinks the impulse to share and circulate problematic content. This is a shift that involves not only *synthetic* media literacy (what deepfakes are) but also *social* media literacy

(Meikle 2016). Such literacies include skills in *accessing*, *interpreting*, and *evaluating* what we encounter in networked digital environments. They involve finding ideas and making meanings from them, and they require an awareness of how digital media and platforms make things available to us (and how they don't). Everyone needs a strong understanding of the roles of software and algorithms in shaping the networked digital media environment that we all now inhabit, and in which deepfakes have established a presence. But there are limits to how much individual responsibility for media literacy we can assign to users in an age of personalized, targeted, algorithmically shared media (Bulger & Davison 2018: 17). As argued above, this really needs changes in the practices of social media platforms too.

Last thoughts

The deepfake examples in the opening paragraph of this book were chosen to give some sense of the range of uses to which synthetic media are being put: art and satire, advocacy and persuasion, influence and porn. The cases to which I've given the most attention are those that I think offer the clearest illustrations of what deepfakes are and of how people are finding ways to use and abuse them. The conceptual art and creative interventions of Bill Posters and Daniel Howe, Stephanie Lepp, and James Coupe. The playful nonsense of 'Sassy Justice' and the radical documentary techniques of *Welcome to Chechnya*. The resurrections of Salvador Dalí and Richard Nixon. The allegations of fakery in volatile political situations in Gabon, Myanmar, or Malaysia, and the warnings of the *risks* of fakery in advocacy campaigns such as those of RepresentUS. And the many thousands of non-consensual deepfake porn videos – we should end on those.

As we have seen throughout this book, deepfakes raise hard questions about consent, from the harvesting of images for use in training machine-learning systems to their uses in conscripting women into porn videos, in satirizing the powerful, in reimagining histories, or in resurrecting the dead. We must not look past these questions of consent. What we settle for now will contribute to shaping how these technologies are developed and deployed in the future. Deepfakes are still very new. Much in the synthetic media arena is still *potential*: a realm of risks and dangers and warnings and possibilities. But the torrent of non-consensual synthetic porn is actual and harmful and real, and it says a lot about how deepfakes have developed so far, and about how much already needs to change.

References

Ajder, H. & Glick, J. (2021) 'Just joking! Deepfakes, satire and the politics of synthetic media', WITNESS and Co-Creation Studio at MIT Documentary Lab, December, https://cocreationstudio.mit.edu/just-joking.

Ajder, H., Patrini, G. & Cavalli, F. (2020) 'Automating image abuse: deepfake bots on Telegram', Sensity, October, https://sensity.ai/reports.

Ajder, H., Patrini, G., Cavalli, F. & Cullen, L. (2019) 'The state of deepfakes: landscape, threats, and impact', Sensity, September, https://sensity.ai/reports.

Alpaydin, E. (2021) *Machine Learning*. Cambridge, MA: MIT Press.

Associated Press (2021) 'Fox News edits video of Biden to make it seem he was being racially insensitive', *Guardian*, 13 November, https://www.theguardian.com/media/2021/nov/13/fox-news-edits-biden-video-negro-leagues-satchel-paige.

Attwood, F. (2018) *Sex Media*. Cambridge: Polity.

Ayyub, R. (2018a) 'I was the victim of a deepfake porn plot intended to silence me', *Huffington Post*, 21 November, https://www.huffingtonpost.co.uk/entry/deepfake-porn_uk_5bf2c126e4b0f32bd58ba316.

References

Ayyub, R. (2018b) 'In India, journalists face slut-shaming and rape threats', *New York Times*, 22 May, https://www.nytimes.com/2018/05/22/opinion/india-journalists-slut-shaming-rape.html.

Ballard, J.G. (1984) 'Introduction to *Crash*, French edition', in Vivian Vale & Andrea Juno (eds), *RE/SEARCH #8/9 J.G. Ballard*. San Francisco: Re/Search, pp. 96–8.

Baraniuk, C. (2018) 'China's Xinhua agency unveils AI news presenter', BBC News, 8 November, https://www.bbc.co.uk/news/technology-46136504.

Baxter, J. (2021) 'How Star Wars deepfake seriously improves Luke Skywalker Cameo in The Mandalorian', Den of Geek, 27 July, https://www.denofgeek.com/tv/star-wars-deepfake-luke-skywalker-mandalorian.

Baym, G. & Jones, J. (eds) (2013) *News Parody and Political Satire across the Globe*. New York: Routledge.

BBC News (2018) 'John F Kennedy's lost speech brought to life', 16 March, https://www.bbc.co.uk/news/uk-scotland-edinburgh-east-fife-43429554.

BBC News (2019) 'Instagram hides likes count in international test "to remove pressure"', 18 July, https://www.bbc.co.uk/news/world-49026935.

BBC News (2020a) 'Pornhub sued by 40 Girls Do Porn sex trafficking victims', 16 December, https://www.bbc.co.uk/news/technology-55333403.

BBC News (2020b) 'Google's Fitbit takeover approved by EU', 17 December, https://www.bbc.co.uk/news/technology-55350796.

Berg, H. (2021) *Porn Work*. Chapel Hill, NC: University of North Carolina Press.

Beschizza, R. (2016) 'Trump slowed 50%', Boing Boing, 19 April, https://boingboing.net/2016/04/19/trump-slowed-50.html.

References

Bickert, M. (2020) 'Enforcing against manipulated media', Meta, 6 January, https://about.fb.com/news/2020/01/enforcing-against-manipulated-media.

Bigsby, C.W.E. (1972) *Dada & Surrealism*. London: Methuen.

Bolter, J.D. & Grusin, R. (1999) *Remediation*. Cambridge, MA: MIT Press.

boyd, d. (2011) 'Social network sites as networked publics: affordances, dynamics, and implications', in Z. Papacharissi (ed.), *A Networked Self*. London: Routledge, pp. 39–58.

boyd, d. (2014) *It's Complicated*. New Haven, CT: Yale University Press.

Briggs, A. & Burke, P., with Ytreberg, E. (2020) *A Social History of the Media* (fourth edition). Cambridge: Polity.

Brooker, J. (2009) 'The polytechnic ghost: Pepper's Ghost, metempsychosis and the magic lantern at the Royal Polytechnic Institution', *Early Popular Visual Culture*, vol. 5, no. 2, pp. 189–206.

Broussard, M. (2018) *Artificial Unintelligence*. Cambridge, MA: MIT Press.

Brown, A.M.L. (2018) 'Videogames and sex', in C. Smith, F. Attwood, with B. McNair (eds), *The Routledge Companion to Media, Sex and Sexuality*. London: Routledge, pp. 239–47.

Brunton, F. & Nissenbaum, H. (2015) *Obfuscation*. Cambridge, MA: MIT Press.

Bucher, T. (2018) *If … Then*. New York: Oxford University Press.

Bulger, M. & Davison, P. (2018) 'The promises, challenges, and futures of media literacy', Data & Society, https://datasociety.net/library/the-promises-challenges-and-futures-of-media-literacy.

Bunz, M. (2019) 'The calculation of meaning: on the

misunderstanding of new artificial intelligence as culture'. *Culture, Theory and Critique*, vol. 60, nos 3–4, pp. 264–78.

Bunz, M. & Meikle, G. (2018) *The Internet of Things*. Cambridge: Polity.

Burgess, J. & Baym, N. (2020) *Twitter: A Biography*. New York: New York University Press.

Burgess, J. & Green, J. (2018) *YouTube* (second edition). Cambridge: Polity.

Burgess, M. (2021) 'The biggest deepfake abuse site is growing in disturbing ways', *Wired*, 15 December, https://www.wired.com/story/deepfake-nude-abuse.

Busse, K. & Lothian, A. (2018) 'A history of slash sexualities', in C. Smith, F. Attwood, with B. McNair (eds), *The Routledge Companion to Media, Sex and Sexuality*. London: Routledge, pp. 117–29.

Cahlan, S. (2020) 'How misinformation helped spark an attempted coup in Gabon', *Washington Post*, 13 February, https://www.washingtonpost.com/politics/2020/02/13/how-sick-president-suspect-video-helped-sparked-an-attempted-coup-gabon.

Carey, J. (1989) *Communication as Culture*. New York: Routledge.

Carmi, E. (2020) *Media Distortions*. New York: Peter Lang.

Castells, M. (2004) *The Power of Identity* (second edition). Oxford: Blackwell.

Cavna, M. (2016) 'One of the best performances in "Rogue One" is by an actor who died in 1994', *Washington Post*, 15 December, https://www.washingtonpost.com/news/comic-riffs/wp/2016/12/15/one-of-the-best-performances-in-rogue-one-is-by-an-actor-who-died-in-1994/.

CDEI (Centre for Data Ethics and Innovation) (2019) 'Snapshot paper – Deepfakes and audiovisual disinformation', 12 September, https://www.gov.uk/government/publications/cdei-publishes-its-first-series-of-three-snapshot-papers-ethical-issues-in-ai/snapshot-paper-deepfakes-and-audiovisual-disinformation.

Chan, J. (2018) 'Violence or pleasure? Surveillance and the (non-)consensual upskirt', *Porn Studies*, vol. 5, no. 3, pp. 351–5.

Chesney, B. & Citron, D. (2019) 'Deep fakes: a looming challenge for privacy, democracy, and national security', *California Law Review*, vol. 107, pp. 1753–820.

Chiu, A. (2019) 'Facebook wouldn't delete an altered video of Nancy Pelosi. What about one of Mark Zuckerberg?', *Washington Post*, 12 June, https://www.washingtonpost.com/nation/2019/06/12/mark-zuckerberg-deepfake-facebook-instagram-nancy-pelosi.

Clarke, A.C. (1999) *Profiles of the Future*. London: Orion.

Cole, S. (2017) 'AI-assisted fake porn is here and we're all fucked', *Motherboard*, 12 November, https://www.vice.com/en/article/gydydm/gal-gadot-fake-ai-porn.

Cole, S. (2019a) 'Girls Do Porn goes to trial over allegations women were tricked into videos', *Motherboard*, 28 June, https://www.vice.com/en/article/3k3wdk/girls-do-porn-goes-to-trial-over-allegations-women-were-tricked-into-videos.

Cole, S. (2019b) 'This horrifying app undresses a photo of any woman with a single click', *Motherboard*, 26 June, https://www.vice.com/en_uk/article/kzm59x/deepnude-app-creates-fake-nudes-of-any-woman.

Cole, S. (2019c) 'This deepfake of Mark Zuckerberg tests Facebook's fake video policies', *Motherboard*, 11 June, https://www.vice.com/en/article/ywyxex/

deepfake-of-mark-zuckerberg-facebook-fake-video-policy.

Cole, S. (2020a) 'The ugly truth behind Pornhub's "Year In Review"', *Motherboard*, 18 February, https://www.vice.com/en/article/wxez8y/pornhub-year-in-review-deepfake.

Cole, S. (2020b) 'Pornhub just purged all unverified content from the platform', *Motherboard*, 14 December, https://www.vice.com/en/article/jgqjjy/pornhub-suspended-all-unverified-videos-content.

Cole, S., Maiberg, E. & Koslerova, A. (2020) '"Frankenstein's monster": images of sexual abuse are fueling algorithmic porn', *Motherboard*, 11 October, https://www.vice.com/en/article/akdgnp/sexual-abuse-fueling-ai-porn-deepfake-czech-casting-girls-do-porn.

Cook, J. (2021) 'A powerful new deepfake tool has digitally undressed thousands of women', *Huffington Post*, 8 November, https://www.huffingtonpost.co.uk/entry/deepfake-tool-nudify-women_n_6112d765e4b005ed49053822.

Coopersmith, J. (1998) 'Pornography, technology and progress,' *Icon*, vol. 4, pp. 94–125.

Cormen, T.H. (2013) *Algorithms Unlocked*. Cambridge, MA: MIT Press.

Coughlan, S. (2020) 'Why did the A-level algorithm say no?', BBC News, 14 August, https://www.bbc.co.uk/news/education-53787203.

Crawford, K. (2021) *Atlas of AI*. New Haven, CT: Yale University Press.

Curran, J. & Seaton, J. (2018) *Power without Responsibility* (eighth edition). London: Routledge.

Dalí Museum (2019a) 'Behind the scenes: Dalí Lives', 8 May, https://www.youtube.com/watch?v=BIDaxl4xqJ4&t.

Dalí Museum (2019b) 'Dalí Lives – art meets artificial

intelligence', 23 January, https://www.youtube.com/watch?v=Okq9zabY8rI.

David, M. (2010) *Peer to Peer and the Music Industry*. London: Sage.

Davis, A. (2019) *Political Communication*. Cambridge: Polity.

Dayan, D. & Katz, E. (1992) *Media Events*. Cambridge, MA: Harvard University Press.

de Seta, G. (2021) '*Huanlian*, or changing faces: deepfakes on Chinese digital media platforms', *Convergence*, vol. 27, no. 4, pp. 935–53.

Debord, G. (1990) *Comments on the Society of the Spectacle* (trans. M. Imrie). London: Verso.

Debord, G. & Wolman, G. (2009) [1956] 'Directions for the use of *détournement*', in D. Evans (ed.), *Appropriation*. London: Whitechapel Gallery, pp. 35–9.

Debusmann, B. (2021) '"Deepfake is the future of content creation"', *BBC News*, 8 March, https://www.bbc.co.uk/news/business-56278411.

DelViscio, J. (2020) 'A Nixon deepfake, a "moon disaster" speech and an information ecosystem at risk', *Scientific American*, 20 July, https://www.scientificamerican.com/article/a-nixon-deepfake-a-moon-disaster-speech-and-an-information-ecosystem-at-risk1.

Delwiche, A. & Henderson, J.J. (eds) (2013) *The Participatory Cultures Handbook*. New York: Routledge

Denham, H. (2020) 'Another fake video of Pelosi goes viral on Facebook', *Washington Post*, 3 August, https://www.washingtonpost.com/technology/2020/08/03/nancy-pelosi-fake-video-facebook.

Desowitz, B. (2019) '"The Irishman": How Industrial Light & Magic's innovative de-aging VFX rescued

Martin Scorsese's mob epic', *IndieWire*, 6 December, https://www.indiewire.com/2019/12/the-irishman-ilm-vfx-de-aging-1202194908.

Devlin, K. (2018) *Turned On*. London: Bloomsbury.

Dickson, A. (2020) 'Synthetic media for good', In Event of Moon Disaster, https://moondisaster.org/synthetic-media-for-good.

Draft Online Safety Bill (2021) Department for Digital, Culture, Media and Sport, 12 May, https://assets.publishing.service.gov.uk/government/uploads/system/uploads/attachment_data/file/985033/Draft_Online_Safety_Bill_Bookmarked.pdf.

Duchamp, M. (1973) 'Apropos of "readymades"', in M. Sanouillet & E. Peterson (eds), *The Writings of Marcel Duchamp*. Boston: Da Capo Press, pp. 141–2.

Dyer, R. (2004) *Heavenly Bodies* (second edition). London: Routledge.

Eisenstein, E. (1983) *The Printing Revolution in Early Modern Europe*. Cambridge: Cambridge University Press.

Elliott, A. (2019) *The Culture of AI*. New York: Routledge.

Elliott, A. (2022) *Making Sense of AI*. Cambridge: Polity.

Elmer-DeWitt, P. (1995) 'Online erotica: on a screen near you', *Time*, 3 July, http://content.time.com/time/subscriber/article/0,33009,983116,00.html.

Ess, C. (2020) *Digital Media Ethics* (third edition). Cambridge: Polity.

Evans, A. (2018) 'Sex and celebrity media', in C. Smith, F. Attwood, with B. McNair (eds), *The Routledge Companion to Media, Sex and Sexuality*. London: Routledge, pp. 248–58.

Evans, D. (ed.) (2009) *Appropriation*. London: Whitechapel Gallery.

Faber, T. (2021) 'VTubers and the women behind the

masks', *Financial Times*, 20 April, https://www.ft.com/content/9d8ec8be-1329-4840-8428-e787058169ff.

Ferguson, K. (2015) 'Everything is a remix [remastered]', https://youtu.be/nJPERZDfyWc.

Fineman, M. (2012) *Faking It*. New York: Metropolitan Museum of Art.

Foucault, M. (1980) 'The eye of power', in C. Gordon (ed.), *Power/Knowledge*. Brighton: Harvester Press, pp. 146–65.

franzke, a.s., Bechmann, A., Zimmer, M., Ess, C. & the Association of Internet Researchers (2020) *Internet Research: Ethical Guidelines 3.0*. https://aoir.org/reports/ethics3.pdf.

Gale, M. (1997) *Dada & Surrealism*. London: Phaidon.

Giansiracusa, N. (2022) 'The destabilizing effects of even low-quality deepfakes', *Slate*, 23 March, https://slate.com/technology/2022/03/zelensky-deepfake-video-surrendering.html.

Gillespie, T. (2014) 'The relevance of algorithms', in T. Gillespie, P. J. Boczkowski & K. A. Foot (eds), *Media Technologies*. Cambridge, MA: MIT Press, pp. 167–93.

Gillespie, T. (2016) 'Algorithm', in B. Peters (ed.), *Digital Keywords*. Princeton, NJ: Princeton University Press, pp. 18–30.

Godwin, R. (2019) 'One giant ... lie? Why so many people still think the moon landings were faked', *Guardian*, 10 July, https://www.theguardian.com/science/2019/jul/10/one-giant-lie-why-so-many-people-still-think-the-moon-landings-were-faked.

Golding, D. (2021) 'The memory of perfection: digital faces and nostalgic franchise cinema', *Convergence*, vol. 27, no. 4, pp. 855–67.

Golingai, P. (2019) 'Is it Azmin or a deepfake?', *The Star* (Malaysia), 15 June, https://www.thestar.com.

References

my/opinion/columnists/one-mans-meat/2019/06/15/
is-it-azmin-or-a-deepfake.

Gorman, A. (2020) 'Kim Kardashian's father resur-
rected as hologram in birthday present from
Kanye West', *Guardian*, 30 October, https://
www.theguardian.com/lifeandstyle/2020/oct/30/
robert-kardashian-resurrected-as-a-hologram-for-
kim-kardashian-wests-birthday.

Graff, R.D. (1956) 'A conversation with Marcel
Duchamp', UbuWeb, https://ubu.com/film/duchamp_
conversation.html.

Gregory, S. (2021a) 'Authoritarian regimes could
exploit cries of "deepfake"', *Wired*, 14 February,
https://www.wired.com/story/opinion-authoritarian-
regimes-could-exploit-cries-of-deepfake.

Gregory, S. (2021b) 'The world needs deepfake experts
to stem this chaos', *Wired*, 24 June, https://www.
wired.com/story/opinion-the-world-needs-deepfake-
experts-to-stem-this-chaos.

Gunkel, D.J. (2016) *Of Remixology*. Cambridge, MA:
MIT Press.

Gunkel, D.J. (2020) *An Introduction to Communication
and Artificial Intelligence*. Cambridge: Polity.

Hall, S. (2019) [1973] 'Encoding and decoding in the
television discourse', in *Essential Essays, Vol. 1*.
Durham, NC: Duke University Press, pp. 257–76.

Hao, K. (2020a) 'Inside the strange new world of being a
deepfake actor', *MIT Technology Review*, 9 October,
https://www.technologyreview.com/2020/10/09/
1009850/ai-deepfake-acting.

Hao, K. (2020b) 'Deepfake Putin is here to warn
Americans about their self-inflicted doom', *MIT
Technology Review*, 29 September, https://www.
technologyreview.com/2020/09/29/1009098/
ai-deepfake-putin-kim-jong-un-us-election.

References

Hartley, J. (2008) *Television Truths*. Malden, MA: Blackwell.

Harwell, D. (2018a) 'White House shares doctored video to support punishment of journalist Jim Acosta', *Washington Post*, 8 November, https://www.washingtonpost.com/technology/2018/11/08/white-house-shares-doctored-video-support-punishment-journalist-jim-acosta.

Harwell, D. (2018b) 'Scarlett Johansson on fake AI-generated sex videos: "Nothing can stop someone from cutting and pasting my image"', *Washington Post*, 31 December, https://www.washingtonpost.com/technology/2018/12/31/scarlett-johansson-fake-ai-generated-sex-videos-nothing-can-stop-someone-cutting-pasting-my-image.

Harwell, D. (2019) 'Faked Pelosi videos, slowed to make her appear drunk, spread across social media', *Washington Post*, 24 May, https://www.washingtonpost.com/technology/2019/05/23/faked-pelosi-videos-slowed-make-her-appear-drunk-spread-across-social-media.

Hayward, P. & Rahn, A. (2015) 'Opening Pandora's Box: pleasure, consent and consequence in the production and circulation of celebrity sex videos', *Porn Studies*, vol. 2, no. 1, pp. 49–61.

Hill, K. (2020) 'The secretive company that might end privacy as we know it', *New York Times*, 18 January, https://www.nytimes.com/2020/01/18/technology/clearview-privacy-facial-recognition.html.

Holliday, C. (2021) 'Rewriting the stars: surface tensions and gender troubles in the online media production of digital deepfakes', *Convergence*, vol. 27, no. 4, pp. 899–918.

Itzkoff, D. (2020) 'The "South Park" guys break down their viral deepfake video', *New York Times*, 29

October, https://www.nytimes.com/2020/10/29/arts/ television/sassy-justice-south-park-deepfake.html.

Jack, C. (2017) 'Lexicon of lies', Data & Society, https://datasociety.net/library/lexicon-of-lies.

Jane, E.A. (2017) *Misogyny online*. London: Sage.

Jenkins, H. (2008) *Convergence Culture* (updated edition). New York: New York University Press.

Jenkins, H., Ito, M. & boyd, d. (2016) *Participatory Culture in a Networked Era*. Cambridge: Polity.

Joho, J. (2020) 'A beginner's guide to the best porn games: what to play and what you should know', Mashable, 10 August, https://mashable.com/article/ best-porn-games-free.

Jurgenson, N. (2019) *The Social Photo*. London: Verso.

Kavka, M. (2018) 'Sex and reality TV', in C. Smith, F. Attwood, with B. McNair (eds), *The Routledge Companion to Media, Sex and Sexuality*. London: Routledge, pp. 309–18.

Kelion, L. (2018) 'Reddit bans deepfake porn videos', BBC News, 7 February, https://www.bbc.co.uk/news/ technology-42984127.

Kelleher, J.D. (2019) *Deep Learning*. Cambridge, MA: MIT Press.

Kitchin, R. (2022) *The Data Revolution* (second edition). London: Sage.

Kristof, N. (2020) 'The children of Pornhub', *New York Times*, 4 December, https://www.nytimes. com/2020/12/04/opinion/sunday/pornhub-rape-trafficking.html.

Kuenzli, R. (2006) *Dada*. London: Phaidon.

Latour, B. (1991) 'Technology is society made durable', in J. Law (ed.), *A Sociology of Monsters*. London: Routledge, pp. 103–31.

Leaver, T., Highfield, T. & Abidin, C. (2020) *Instagram*. Cambridge: Polity.

References

LeCun, Y., Bengio, Y. & Hinton, G. (2015) 'Deep learning', *Nature*, vol. 521, pp. 436–44.

Lessig, L. (1999) *Code and Other Laws of Cyberspace*. New York: Basic Books.

Lessig, L. (2004) *Free Culture*. New York: Penguin.

Lessig, L. (2008) *Remix*. London: Bloomsbury Academic.

Levenson, M. (2020) 'Judge awards nearly $13 million to women who say they were exploited by porn producers', *New York Times*, 2 January, https://www.nytimes.com/2020/01/02/us/girls-do-porn-lawsuit-award.html.

Longstaff, G. (2018) 'Celebrity sex tapes', in C. Smith, F. Attwood, with B. McNair (eds), *The Routledge Companion to Media, Sex and Sexuality*. London: Routledge, pp. 183–92.

Losh, E. (2020) *Hashtag*. New York: Bloomsbury Academic.

Lupton, D. (2020) *Data Selves*. Cambridge: Polity.

Lyon, D. (2018) *The Culture of Surveillance*. Cambridge: Polity.

Manovich, L. (2001) *The Language of New Media*. Cambridge, MA: MIT Press.

Manovich, L. (2006) 'Generation Flash', in W.H.K. Chun & T. Keenan (eds), *New Media, Old Media*. New York: Routledge, pp. 209–18.

Manovich, L. (2007) 'What comes after remix?', http://manovich.net/index.php/projects/what-comes-after-remix.

Manovich, L. (2013) *Software Takes Command*. New York: Bloomsbury.

Marcus, G. (1989) *Lipstick Traces*. London: Picador.

Martin, J., Haberman, M. & Burns, A. (2017) 'Why Trump stands by Roy Moore, even as it fractures his party', *New York Times*, 25 November, https://

www.nytimes.com/2017/11/25/us/politics/trump-roy-moore-mcconnell-alabama-senate.html.

Martin, N. (2017) 'Online predators spread fake porn of me. Here's how I fought back', TED, November, https://www.ted.com/talks/noelle_martin_online_predators_spread_fake_porn_of_me_here_s_how_i_fought_back.

Marvin, C. (1988) *When Old Technologies Were New*. New York: Oxford University Press.

Marwick, A. & Lewis, R. (2017) 'Media manipulation and disinformation online', Data & Society, https://datasociety.net/library/media-manipulation-and-disinfo-online.

Massanari, A. (2017) '#Gamergate and The Fappening: how Reddit's algorithm, governance, and culture support toxic technocultures', *New Media & Society*, vol. 19, no. 3, pp. 329–46.

McEwan, P. (2015) *The Birth of a Nation*. London: Palgrave/British Film Institute.

McGlynn, C. & Rackley, E. (2017) 'Image-based sexual abuse', *Oxford Journal of Legal Studies*, vol. 37, no. 3, pp. 534–61.

McNair, B. (2018) *Fake News*. London: Routledge.

Meikle, G. (2002) *Future Active*. New York: Routledge.

Meikle G. (2007) 'Stop signs: an introduction to culture jamming', in K. Coyer, T. Dowmunt & A. Fountain (eds), *The Alternative Media Handbook*. London: Routledge, pp. 166–79.

Meikle, G. (2008) 'Whacking Bush: tactical media as play', in M. Boler (ed.), *Digital Media and Democracy*. Cambridge, MA: MIT Press, pp. 367–82.

Meikle, G. (2016) *Social Media*. New York: Routledge.

Meikle, G. & Young, S. (2012) *Media Convergence*. Basingstoke: Palgrave Macmillan.

Meta AI (2020) 'Deepfake detection challenge results:

an open initiative to advance AI', 12 June, https:// ai.facebook.com/blog/deepfake-detection-challenge- results-an-open-initiative-to-advance-ai.

Meta Platforms, Inc. (2022) *Annual Report*, 3 February, https://investor.fb.com/financials/default.aspx.

Metz, C. (2019) 'A fake Zuckerberg video challenges Facebook's rules', *New York Times*, 11 June, https:// www.nytimes.com/2019/06/11/technology/fake- zuckerberg-video-facebook.html.

Meyrowitz, J. (1985) *No Sense of Place*. New York: Oxford University Press.

Mihailova, M. (2021) 'To dally with Dalí: deepfake (inter)faces in the art museum', *Convergence*, vol. 27, no. 4, pp. 882–98.

Miller, P.D. (2004) *Rhythm Science*. Cambridge, MA: MIT Press.

Mirsky, Y. & Lee, W. (2020) 'The creation and detection of deepfakes: a survey'. *ACM Computing Surveys*, vol. 54, no. 1, article 7.

Murphie, A. & Potts, J. (2003) *Culture and Technology*. Basingstoke: Palgrave Macmillan.

Natale, S. (2021) *Deceitful Media*. New York: Oxford University Press.

Navas, E. (2012) *Remix Theory*. New York: Springer-Verlag/Wien.

Navas, E., Gallagher, O. & burrough, x. (2015a) 'Introduction', in E. Navas, O. Gallagher & x. burrough (eds), *The Routledge Companion to Remix Studies*. New York: Routledge, pp. 1–12.

Navas, E., Gallagher, O. & burrough, x. (eds) (2015b) *The Routledge Companion to Remix Studies*. New York: Routledge.

Navas, E., Gallagher, O. & burrough, x. (eds) (2018) *Keywords in Remix Studies*. New York: Routledge.

New York Times (2016) 'Transcript: Donald Trump's

taped comments about women', 8 October, https://www.nytimes.com/2016/10/08/us/donald-trump-tape-transcript.html.

Noble, S.U. (2018) *Algorithms of Oppression*. New York: New York University Press.

Ofcom (2021) *Online Nation: 2021 Report*, 9 June, https://www.ofcom.org.uk/__data/assets/pdf_file/0013/220414/online-nation-2021-report.pdf.

O'Neil, C. (2016) *Weapons of Math Destruction*. New York: Crown.

O'Neil, L. (2019) 'Doctored video of sinister Mark Zuckerberg puts Facebook to the test', *Guardian*, 12 June, https://www.theguardian.com/technology/2019/jun/11/deepfake-zuckerberg-instagram-facebook.

Ong, T. (2020) 'Virtual influencers make real money while Covid locks down human stars', *Bloomberg Businessweek*, 29 October, https://www.bloomberg.com/news/features/2020-10-29/lil-miquela-lol-s-seraphine-virtual-influencers-make-more-real-money-than-ever.

O'Sullivan, D (2020) 'Another fake Pelosi video goes viral on Facebook', CNN, 3 August, https://edition.cnn.com/2020/08/02/politics/fake-nancy-pelosi-video-facebook/index.html.

Paasonen, S. (2018a) 'Online pornography', in N. Brügger & I. Milligan (eds), *The Sage Handbook of Web History*. London: Sage, pp. 551–63.

Paasonen, S. (2018b) 'User-generated pornography', in C. Smith, F. Attwood, with B. McNair (eds), *The Routledge Companion to Media, Sex and Sexuality*. London: Routledge, pp. 174–82.

Paasonen, S., Jarrett, K. & Light, B. (2019) *NSFW*. Cambridge, MA: MIT Press.

Panetta, F. & Burgund, H. (2020) 'Why we made

this deepfake', *In Event of Moon Disaster*, https://moondisaster.org/why-we-made-this-deepfake.

Paris, B. & Donovan, J. (2019) 'Deepfakes and cheap fakes', Data & Society, https://datasociety.net/library/deepfakes-and-cheap-fakes.

Patrini, G. (2021) 'The state of deepfakes 2020: update on statistics and trends', Sensity, March, http://www.sensity.ai/reports.

Paul, K. (2020) 'Pornhub removes millions of videos after investigation finds child abuse content', *Guardian*, 14 December, https://www.theguardian.com/technology/2020/dec/14/pornhub-purge-removes-unverified-videos-investigation-child-abuse.

Penley, C. (1991) 'Brownian motion: women, tactics, and technology', in C. Penley & A. Ross (eds), *Technoculture*. Minneapolis: University of Minnesota Press, pp. 135–61

Pesenti, J. (2021) 'An update on our use of face recognition', Meta, 2 November, https://about.fb.com/news/2021/11/update-on-use-of-face-recognition.

Pierson, M. (2002) *Special Effects*. New York: Columbia University Press.

Poole, C. (2010) 'The case for anonymity online', TED, February, https://www.ted.com/talks/christopher_moot_poole_the_case_for_anonymity_online?language=en.

Popova, M. (2020) 'Reading out of context: pornographic deepfakes, celebrity and intimacy', *Porn Studies*, vol. 7, no. 4, pp. 367–81.

Pornhub Insights (2019a) 'Avengers search popularity', 23 April, https://www.pornhub.com/insights/avengers-2019.

Pornhub Insights (2019b) 'The 2019 year in review', 11 December, https://www.pornhub.com/insights/2019-year-in-review#celebrity.

References

Pornhub Insights (2021) 'The Pornhub tech review', 8 April, https://www.pornhub.com/insights/tech-review.

Posters, B. (2021a) 'From synthetic media to synthetic art', talk presented at Aesthetica Art Prize 'Future Now' Symposium, 1 May, https://aestheticamagazine.com/future-now-symposium-2021.

Posters, B. (2021b) 'Foundation Series', http://billposters.ch/projects/foundation-series-2021.

Posters, B. & Howe, D. (2019a) 'Data is ...', Vimeo, https://vimeo.com/341904916.

Posters, B. & Howe, D. (2019b) 'Big Dada/Public Faces', http://billposters.ch/projects/big-dada.

Posters, B. & Howe, D. (2019c) 'Gallery: "Spectre" launches (press release)', http://billposters.ch/spectre-launch.

Postman, N. & Paglia, C. (2007) [1991] 'Two cultures – television versus print', in D. Crowley & P. Heyer (eds), *Communication in History* (fifth edition). Boston: Allyn & Bacon, pp. 283–95.

Raji, I.D. & Fried, G. (2021) 'About face: a survey of facial recognition evaluation', https://arxiv.org/pdf/2102.00813.pdf.

Rasula, J. (2015) *Destruction Was My Beatrice*. New York: Basic Books.

Reuters News Agency (2019) *Identifying and Tackling Manipulated Media*, https://www.reuters.com/manipulatedmedia.

Ribeiro, C. (2019) 'How turning "likes" invisible is changing Instagram', BBC Worklife, 23 August, https://www.bbc.com/worklife/article/20190822-how-turning-likes-invisible-is-changing-instagram.

Ronson, J. (2017) 'Episode 1: A nondescript building in Montreal', *The Last Days of August*. https://podcasts.apple.com/gb/podcast/the-last-days-of-august/id1258779354?i=1000394362874.

References

Rosen, J. (2006) 'The people formerly known as the audience', PressThink, 27 June, http://archive. pressthink.org/2006/06/27/ppl_frmr.html.

Rosner, H. (2021) 'The ethics of a deepfake Anthony Bourdain voice', *New Yorker*, 17 July, https://www.newyorker.com/culture/annals-of-gastronomy/the-ethics-of-a-deepfake-anthony-bourdain-voice.

Russell, B. (2015) 'Appropriation is activism', in E. Navas, O. Gallagher & x. burrough (eds), *The Routledge Companion to Remix Studies*. New York: Routledge, pp. 217–23.

Schick, N. (2020) *Deepfakes and the Infocalypse*. London: Monoray.

Seaver, N. (2019) 'Knowing algorithms', in J. Vertesi & D. Ribes (eds), *digitalSTS*. Princeton, NJ: Princeton University Press, pp. 412–22.

Senate Committee on the Judiciary (US) (2021) *Subverting Justice*, 7 October, https://www.judiciary. senate.gov/press/dem/releases/following-8-month-investigation-senate-judiciary-committee-releases-report-on-donald-trumps-scheme-to-pressure-doj-and-overturn-the-2020-election.

Senft, T. (2008) *Camgirls*. New York: Peter Lang.

Seymour, M. (2019) 'Canny AI: imagine world leaders singing', fxguide, 12 April, https://www.fxguide. com/fxfeatured/canny-ai-imagine-world-leaders-singing.

Shand-Baptiste, K. (2019) 'Zuckerberg must tolerate the deepfake treatment – and it's all thanks to Facebook's shoddy approach to news', *Independent*, 12 June, https://www.independent.co.uk/voices/facebook-mark-zuckerberg-video-deepfake-pelosi-social-media-a8955441.html.

Simonite, T. (2021) 'Are these the hidden deepfakes in the Anthony Bourdain movie?', *Wired*, 23 August, https://

www.wired.com/story/these-hidden-deepfakes-anthony-bourdain-movie.

Simonite, T. (2022) 'A Zelensky deepfake was quickly defeated. The next one might not be', *Wired*, 17 March, https://www.wired.com/story/zelensky-deepfake-facebook-twitter-playbook.

Sinnreich, A. (2010) *Mashed Up*. Amherst: University of Massachusetts Press.

Snapes, L. (2019) 'Amy Winehouse hologram tour postponed due to "unique sensitivities"', *Guardian*, 22 February, https://www.theguardian.com/music/2019/feb/22/amy-winehouse-hologram-tour-postponed.

St Michel, P. (2016) 'A brief history of virtual pop stars', *Pitchfork*, 15 July, https://pitchfork.com/thepitch/1229-a-brief-history-of-virtual-pop-stars.

Stella, R. (2016) 'The amateur roots of gonzo pornography', *Porn Studies*, vol. 3, no. 4, pp. 351–61.

Stupp, C. (2019) 'Fraudsters used AI to mimic CEO's voice in unusual cybercrime case', *Wall Street Journal*, 30 August, https://www.wsj.com/articles/fraudsters-use-ai-to-mimic-ceos-voice-in-unusual-cybercrime-case-11567157402.

Sullivan, R. & McKee, A. (2015) *Pornography*. Cambridge: Polity.

Swaine, J. (2018) 'Trump inauguration crowd photos were edited after he intervened', *Guardian*, 6 September, https://www.theguardian.com/world/2018/sep/06/donald-trump-inauguration-crowd-size-photos-edited.

Thompson, J.B. (1995) *The Media and Modernity*. Cambridge: Polity.

Thompson, J.B. (2000) *Political Scandal*. Cambridge: Polity.

Thomson, P. (2020) 'Digital disguise: "Welcome to Chechnya"'s face veil is a game changer in identity protection', International Documentary Association, 30 June, https://www.documentary.org/column/digital-disguise-welcome-chechnyas-face-veil-game-changer-identity-protection.

Turner, G. (2010) *Ordinary People and the Media.* London: Sage.

Twitter, Inc. (2022) *Annual Report: Fiscal Year 2021,* 16 February, https://investor.twitterinc.com/financial-information/default.aspx.

van der Nagel, E. (2020) 'Verifying images: deepfakes, control, and consent', *Porn Studies*, vol. 7, no. 4, pp. 424–9.

Vaneigem, R. (1983) [1967]. *The Revolution of Everyday Life.* London: Rebel Press and Left Bank Books.

Venkataramakrishnan, S. (2021) 'Behind the Tom Cruise deepfakes that can evade disinformation tools', *Financial Times*, 5 March, https://www.ft.com/content/721da1df-a1e5-4e2f-97fe-6de633ed4826.

Verdegem, P. (2021) 'Introduction: Why we need critical perspectives on AI', in P. Verdegem (ed.), *AI for Everyone?* London: University of Westminster Press, pp. 1–18.

Vermorel, F. (1985) *Starlust.* London: Faber.

Wahl-Jorgensen, K. (2019) *Emotions, Media and Politics.* Cambridge: Polity.

Wakefield, J. (2021) 'MP Maria Miller wants AI "nudifying" tool banned', BBC News, 4 August, https://www.bbc.co.uk/news/technology-57996910.

Wakefield, J. (2022) 'Deepfake presidents used in Russia–Ukraine war', *BBC News,* 18 March, https://www.bbc.co.uk/news/technology-60780142.

Waldersee, V. (2019) 'Which science-based conspiracy theories do Britons believe?', YouGov, 25 April, https://yougov.co.uk/topics/science/articles-reports/2019/04/25/which-science-based-conspiracy-theories-do-britons.

Wardle, C. (2020) 'Journalism and the new information ecoystem: responsibilities and challenges', in M. Zimdars & K. McLeod (eds), *Fake News*. Cambridge, MA: MIT Press, pp. 71–85.

Wardle, C. & Derakhshan, H. (2017) *Information Disorder: Toward an Interdisciplinary Framework for Research And Policymaking*, https://firstdraftnews.com/wp-content/uploads/2017/11/PREMS-162317-GBR-2018-Report-de%CC%81sinformation-1.pdf?x56713.

Wark, M. (2012) *Telesthesia*. Cambridge: Polity.

Warwick, K. (2012) *Artificial Intelligence*. London: Routledge.

Washington Post (2020) 'White House social media director tweets manipulated video to depict Biden asleep in TV interview', 3 September, https://www.washingtonpost.com/video/politics/white-house-social-media-director-tweets-manipulated-video-to-depict-biden-asleep-in-tv-interview/2020/09/02/4c71391a-44bd-40e0-91ab-e98077e9b17b_video.html.

Weiser, M. (1991) 'The computer for the 21st century', *Scientific American*, September, pp. 94–104.

Wesch, M. (2009) 'YouTube and you: experiences of self-awareness in the context collapse of the recording webcam', *Explorations in Media Ecology*, vol. 8, no. 2, pp. 19–34.

Winner, L. (1986) *The Whale and the Reactor*. Chicago: University of Chicago Press.

WITNESS (2018) 'Summary of discussions and next step recommendations from "Mal-uses of AI-generated synthetic media and deepfakes: pragmatic solutions discovery convening"', 11 June, http://witness.

mediafire.com/file/q5juw7dc3a2w8p7/Deepfakes_
Final.pdf/fil.

WITNESS (2020a) 'Memory, archives, history and
deepfakes: Francesca Panetta, Halsey Burgund, James
Coupe, Yvonne Ng', 5 October, https://www.youtube.
com/watch?v=PQVFgqHAZ5M.

WITNESS (2020b) 'Identity protection with
deepfakes: "Welcome to Chechnya" director David
France', 14 September, https://www.youtube.com/
watch?v=2du6dVL3Nuc.

WITNESS (2021) 'Just joking? Deepfakes, satire, and
the politics of synthetic media', 8 November, https://
www.youtube.com/watch?v=QNBV-ZkeMcc.

Witt, S. (2015) *How Music Got Free*. New York:
Viking.

Woodhouse, J. (2021) 'Regulating online harms', House
of Commons Library Research Briefing, 12 August,
https://commonslibrary.parliament.uk/research-
briefings/cbp-8743.

Woodward, B. & Bernstein, C. (1974) *All The President's
Men*. London: Secker & Warburg.

Zecca, F. (2018) 'Ways of showing it', in C. Smith,
F. Attwood, with B. McNair (eds), *The Routledge
Companion to Media, Sex and Sexuality*. London:
Routledge, pp. 141–50.

Zimdars, M. & McLeod, K. (eds) (2020) *Fake News*.
Cambridge, MA: MIT Press.

Zucconi, A. (2018) 'An introduction to deepfakes',
https://www.alanzucconi.com/2018/03/14/
introduction-to-deepfakes.

Index

Index

Index

189

Index

190